# SYLVIA LERO

# Barefoot Roving

## The Travelling Kitchen

## Fremantle Arts Centre Press

*Australia's finest small publisher*

# Contents

I would like to formally dedicate this book to Tim Jones aboard the Wharram cat *Quirky*,

Steve Boase aboard the Wharram cat *Banana Mousskourri*,

the memory of Dave Legge aboard the Wharram cat *Juringa*,

and all those who sail free.

# Preface

Bookstores around Australia are crowded with recipe books addressing an impressive variety of cuisines, nutritional aspirations, budgets and special circumstances. However, even the most dedicated publication for the challenge of cooking at sea — as I do — or for those caravanning or camping light, seems to take it for granted that there is refrigeration, or that you are travelling in near-polar latitudes, or that you are content to eat out of tins and freeze-dried packets of processed food.

*Barefoot Roving Cookbook* is an attempt to fill the gap, and explain how to meet the needs of a hungry mob while sailing, touring or holidaying, without the benefit of refrigeration and far from supermarkets and takeaways. It also offers information on methods of preserving and maximising yields for hobby farmers and cottage garden enthusiasts; information which was commonplace just a few generations ago, but has been eclipsed by today's consumer society.

Fresh greens can be grown and gathered, fresh bread baked with wild yeast, fresh yoghurt and curds brewed daily, and fresh fish can be pickled and soused. Moreover, we can leave remote places as we found them, not littered with tins, bottles and plastic packaging.

Not only seafarers like me need this information; these ideas fall easily within the scope of a range of barefoot rovers — the practical homemaker striving for a greener lifestyle, the caravanner, the off-road camper with limited refrigeration. Even if every single one of the millions of pleasure craft afloat in Australian waters and caravans making their way around the continent today has a fridge or esky on board, I'll bet every skipper would gladly see that fridge reserved for cold drinks!

Contemporary sophisticated navigation equipment — the Global Positioning System, or GPS — is now commonplace on even the smallest trailer-sailer. With its blistering accuracy, ordinary people are confidently venturing further into more remote areas. That means the need to manage food better for longer is greater. It also implies a parallel need for ordinary people to gain more self-reliance the further they rove from community back-up.

As a cookbook, *Barefoot Roving* is conspicuously and unashamedly narrow in focus. My intension is to reveal (or re-expose) old skills to avoid the burden of heavy, cumbersome and expensive stores such as tins and bottles, packets and mixes of prepared food. Fresher food can be had on a shoestring. A few staples like salt, sugar, spice, flour and fat will keep you content in isolated places, with the dedicated confidence of a broody hen settled on a clutch of eggs. All the recipes are designed to be executed in a typical galley, although they can also be prepared on shore and carried on to the boat.

# Author's Note

Fresh eggs, milk and butter aren't always available to the barefoot rover. When butter is listed as an ingredient in any recipe, ghee can equally be used. Similarly, if a recipe calls for milk, powdered milk (and often liquid bread-sour) can be substituted. With a few exceptions (noted in the recipes), eggs can be replaced by the substitutes described on page 46.

A guide to the measures used and metric/imperial conversion tables are on page 251.

# An Introduction to Barefoot Cruising

In our so-called 'free' society, freedom is a sadly diminishing thing. We should know that freedom does not exist without responsibility, for then it becomes mere self-indulgence. In an apparent unwillingness to shoulder that basic and precious responsibility, we allow our lives to be cluttered more and more with regulations and 'safeguards' which really just shuffle the responsibility into the hands of various authorities.

In house construction today for instance, the main building component is Red Tape, and there seems to be a yawning gulf between a dwelling that is spiritually, ethically and permaculturally wholesome and the sort of dwelling that the authorities will permit. Yet it is still possible to build something that will stay afloat in water, call it a boat, and be free to live on board. Boats are one of the last bastions of freedom from the constraints of authority.

But whether it is under sail or on the road, the term barefoot rover describes those people who set out to enjoy their environment with the intention of making minimal impact on the natural assets of this globe we all call home. A great fraternity has built up amongst such barefoot travellers, men and women who share information about safe anchorages and good camping grounds, the pleasures and hazards of various areas, and the last-known whereabouts of various fellow travellers. In the boating fraternity — and it must be obvious by now that it is from this fraternity that I mainly speak — they avidly exchange information on such vital subjects as a sailmaker with her sewing machine aboard somebody's boat in the next port north, or a solar power guru on so-and-so's vessel heading south, unexpected weather patterns, or just a new recipe for fruitcake or home brew.

Any day of the week, great numbers of barefoot rovers may be found messing about in sailing boats, spending weekends and weeks and months nosing along the coast, island-hopping or even making ocean passages. Typically, these people choose to be as self-reliant as possible, and the more they get a taste of the freedom and satisfaction this attitude engenders the more likely they are to abandon shore life, 'run away to sea' and live aboard their boat.

In the boating world where precious freedom is greater, responsibility is greater too. Barefoot cruisers cherish their freedom and most of them readily acknowledge their responsibilities. Responsible for themselves, they prepare for the worst and enjoy the best. The least you can do for yourself is also the best you can do.

*

A great champion of the barefoot roving lifestyle was the late Dave Legge aboard the Wharram catamaran *Juringa* VNQ 2323. Dave finally lost his battle with cancer in September 2003, but remained defiantly aboard his spartan home right up to the last week of his life. *Juringa* is a 36-foot cutter rigged ketch, with beautifully carved stem-posts depicting Polynesian figureheads; curved cabin tops and a huge, imposing brass compass roughly the same age as the skipper in his last years, about seventy-five in the shade.

Any excuse was enough for Dave to up-anchor and sail — sail anywhere, sail just to give a total stranger the experience of sailing, or to meet friends for a beach picnic and barbecue in the Montebellos or the Buccaneer Archipelago or wherever.

In his commitment to keeping *Juringa* as light as possible — so that her sailing performance would be maximised — Dave chose to lash a sweep oar to the deck as auxiliary, rather than own an outboard. He also selected paperback books for his library rather than hard-covers, carried the barest minimum of clothes, and used kero lamps and a metho stove to avoid cumbersome gas bottles or heavy batteries and solar panels. Preparing to cruise out to the Buccaneers once, he said, 'Two pencils for navigation? What do we need two pencils for? That's too heavy! If we have two pencils we'll never know where either of them are, but if we just have one pencil we know we must look after it.' Like all good barefoot rovers he sailed by dead reckoning and only switched on his battery-operated GPS to confirm his position.

On one adventure when conditions had been so inclement that the main boom snapped, Dave discarded the boom and rigged the main as a loose-footed sail, very happy to have lessened the weight and improved safety at the same time. He never replaced the boom, but said he would allow me to make a rolling pin out of a section of it for the galley!

*

Barefoot roving is not a new concept but rather a return to old ways and the wisdom of earlier generations. We don't have to be Flinders or King to prove that this island Australia is circumnavigable, but neither do we need to rely on anything more than the wind to make that journey. Fossil fuels can stay in the ground in favour of renewable energy as far as barefoot rovers are concerned.

Truly dedicated cruisers stand apart from the rest of the boating world. People like Conrad Jelinek aboard the bijou *Carousa*, a 1932 Hillyard cutter, 30' x 9'6" x 4'9", pitch pine on English oak and Honduras mahogany, with a black iron keel, and one genuine Rolls Royce light switch. Such people have an admirable understanding of freedom and what makes life truly valuable. They have pared down their life's possessions, understanding that most material things are straws in the wind at which we clutch in vain, giving only a false sense of security. As if in counterbalance, people like Conrad have intensified their appreciation and enjoyment of fundamental things like good company and good food.

I met Conrad in Ulladulla, when I was custodian of the William Fyfe sloop *Carina* (one does not ever 'own' such a creature). He had promised me a guitar recital but a change in the wind meant that he headed north earlier than planned. He sent, instead — *par voilier* of course — a copy of a poem he had written in celebration of surviving a perilous night passage.

With his wife and child, Conrad had sailed the seven seas with a metho stove, no fridge, and a radio-receiver but no transmitter. *Carousa* had been their home for ten years or more, and the locker doors in the galley were beautifully decorated with paintings of sea creatures, genuine folk-art.

Similarly, the Ericsson sloop *Aku Ankka* is the permanent home of Glen Horne and Erja Vasumaki, well-known contributors to cruising magazines, who, after twelve years, non-stop cruising still had no fridge on board. An ongoing project for Erja is the creation of a colourful quilt, each panel recording memorable events of their endless cruise, one a rainbow sewn by Erja's daughter.

In the days before Emergency Position Indicator Repeater Beacons (EPIRBs) or the Global Positioning System (GPS), Steve 'Sailor' Abney spent nine years crossing the Pacific, solo, and had survived a cyclone at sea. I met him when he sold me the Finnish sloop *Brita*. Launched in 1948, *Brita* measured 38'x 9'x 6' and had a Baltic pine carvel hull, black iron keel and massive iron floors. Steve had been a US navy frogman in the Vietnam War. He told me that he never set out on an ocean passage without six months' supply of stores on board, mostly beans stowed in plastic drums.

Of a somewhat different philosophy was Kelvin Jacoby, one of the wilder barefoot cruisers I have met. In September 1986 he set sail from Ulladulla in his 18-foot fibreglass sloop. His tender, a surfboard, had been pinched, so he said it was time to go. With no compass, no log, no GPS, no autohelm, no engine and no safety gear, he loaded 12 gallons of drinking water, a carton of salted potato chip packs, and a bloody big bag of barley sugar and spent the next nineteen days crossing the Tasman Sea to New Zealand to visit his son. And he got there safely, unassisted.

*

Of course it is possible to flash the plastic and be at the helm of a high-tech, state-of-the-art cruiser: fuel-hungry, eutectic-frozen, air-conditioned, microwaved, fully electric, equipped to go anywhere ... 'State of the art'! What art? Con art! Big business would have us believe we cannot survive without over-consuming their mass productions. Don't be conned into believing that luxuries are essentials. They are complications more likely. Commonsense tells you that the simpler your outfit the easier it will be to care for, repair or replace. If the boat you have chartered includes all those dazzling extras, you are not compelled to use them!

Among too many of today's travellers on boats and in caravans, the burning questions concern where can they find a good refrigeration mechanic; where can they refuel or restock from fancy delicatessen stores. Soon these necessities fester into gripes and grumbles about how heavy and expensive they are, a sad lament because they are unnecessary if people would simply unravel the complications of a cruising galley.

In his ballad 'Come by Chance' Banjo Paterson reminds us:

> ... *all that makes this life worth living*
> *Comes unstriven for, and free.*

We need our eyes open to the things that make this life worth living.

*

Barefoot roving celebrates a revival of old values, including reverence for food and respect for the essential elements of pride and time in food preparation. From this perspective, food preparation is not a chore, but a satisfaction akin to playing music, as distinct from listening to music being played. It encompasses a spiritual satisfaction incomprehensible to those who have never experienced it. Whether you are at sea or on land, my strongest recommendation to you is this: put the power of food preparation back into your own grasp, where it belongs.

Our forebears, black and white, were survivors. They slaughtered their own meat, ground their own grain and prepared their own food. I believe the spiritual dignity of self-respect was theirs through such work. No one possessing self-respect can rightly be described as impoverished.

Our contemporaries, handicapped by fast food and consumerism, are so spiritually impoverished they are dying by suicide at a rate higher than ever before recorded. They are not even survivors.

My advice to my contemporaries is to revive some of the skills and values of earlier generations, starting with food. Let 'success' take on a deeper meaning, in which the 'perfection' of processed or manufactured food is seen for what it really is — bland and monotonous, not success at all. If your jam doesn't set, don't call it a failure — call it fruit salad sauce. If your first steak and kidney pie turns out to be a mistake and kidney pie, who cares? As one of Sir Edmund Hillary's climbers on Everest said: 'The only really important thing about food is that there should BE SOME!'

A recipe is a guide, not a rigid formula but a skeleton of proportions, ratios.

volume : time

wet : dry

fat : flour

temperature : result


Everything else is your own cadenza. It can be a breathtaking diapason of flavours and textures or a simple rustic folk melody. You are the orchestrator.

*

In a world of diminishing resources, poverty and increasing mouths to be fed, the worst crime of the affluent against humanity must be the wasting of food, closely followed by the next worst crime: the squandering of other vital resources. These are not crimes of which only the affluent are guilty, but the affluent, presumably, have the benefit of more education, and therefore fewer excuses. It bears repeating: to me, education means understanding that privilege equals duty. If I am privileged enough to have a boat of my own, and untroubled waters in which to cruise, then it is my duty to protect that environment.

On one very memorable trip aboard the *Juringa*, sheltering inside Dirk Hartog Island, two of the crew went ashore with the red cloud sheepdog Maggot and a pocket-knife. They returned with fresh goat's milk and three feral goats. Being thoroughly responsible barefoot rovers they had obtained permission from the ranger to slaughter the goats. The challenge then was to preserve this welcome bounty on a fridge-free vessel. The skins were used as baggy wrinkles in the rigging (for non-yachties, baggy wrinkles protect the sails from chafing caused by the standing-rigging), and the mizzen boom was hung with hindquarters (wrapped in cheesecloth) that would be used immediately in stews and roasts.

The meat from the forequarters we cut into narrow strips which we steeped overnight in a dry mixture of curry powder and cooking salt. Next morning much of the moisture in the meat had been extracted by the salt and spices, and I used a sail needle to thread the strips of meat onto lengths of fishing line and hung them in the rigging. A single day spent hanging in the cold and ceaseless wind of that latitude was enough to render the biltong ready to store in jars for later use in curry or as snack food — chewy, delicious and sustaining, free from genetic engineering and chemicals. Department of Conservation and Land Management had planned simply to destroy the goats, at the loss of all those resources.

*

Many of us feel dejected and frail in the face of the sheer magnitude of all the world's bad news hurled at us every day — political and social as well as environmental travesties. Take heart! Think globally and act locally. Eat simply, so that others may simply eat. Even the simplest action generates a reaction. The choice begins with our individual selves, and the outcome is the cumulative result of each individual choice.

We can take pride in taking responsibility. Self-respect is perhaps our most valuable asset, certainly one of the things that make life worth living. And we can start now, with the greening of our own galley skills for the most important essential of our own life: our own sustenance, both spiritual and physical. In this book I will share with you some commonsense ideas on how to manage food and thrive in tropical cruising grounds, where twentieth century fuel is unavailable, credit cards are just so much ballast, shops and mail services are far over the horizon, and your ravenous crew are licking their lips at meal-times.

Before stepping into the galley though, the next chapter introduces my cruising grounds and the Wharram catamaran *Banana Mousskourri*, while 'Roving Profile' traces some family history that helps explain my enthusiasm for recipes and for the sea.

# The Kimberley, Broome & Banana Mousskourri

Cruising in a tropical climate lends itself to a leisurely daily pattern. The length of the day varies little between seasons. Most people fall into the habit of rising early for breakfast in the coolest hour before dawn. Next comes a mid-morning meal before the hottest hours. Nothing stirs in the lethargy of a tropical midday, and by mid-afternoon everyone's looking for lots of drinks and light refreshment. After dark, when bush flies and mozzies have given up the game, a last meal is served, cocooned in the silken warmth of a tropical night, under a Kimberley moon.

*

The Kimberley coast offers countless secret spots for secluded anchorages among unnamed islands with untrodden beaches, where sleeping on deck is as natural as the waxing and waning of the moon.

My particular cruising grounds extend well beyond the Kimberley, from 18°S on the west coast, across the 'top' of the 900 nautical miles of Northern Territory coast, and around to Cairns and Lucinda at 18°S on the eastern Queensland coast. In total, close to 2,700 nautical miles of remote country, an extent dwarfing Texas.

For the tropical barefoot rover it is an area of extremes: extreme tidal range and extreme heat and humidity. It is a vast area, as timeless and haunting as the thrum of the didgeridoo; isolated, challenging, spell-binding and unforgiving — a place about which you can become passionate. This place forges people, while the land itself remains steadfastly unmalleable.

The rips, whirlpools, and horizontal waterfalls which feature in so many tourist brochures must have been breathtaking, awe-inspiring discoveries in Captain King's day aboard the little *Mermaid* in 1820, as he made the first detailed charts of this coast. Life-saving information, such as the abundance of fresh water at Mermaid Island, which King drew onto his chart, and which was included on the old admiralty fathom charts, is strangely no longer to be found in the metric charts provided by the authorities today. The same authorities have turned out many of the coastal navigation lights, and 'automated' those that remain, a sad loss.

On the marine chart the Kimberley port of Broome lies at Lat. 17.59 S Long. 122.12 E. In the early twentieth century up to 400 pearling luggers worked out of Broome in any one season, sailing these Kimberley waters, gathering wild pearl shell, the *Pinctada maxima*. Here were all the flotsam and jetsam of the gold-rush era, runaway sailors, do-gooders, adventurers, and entrepreneurs from many nations. Broome was a thriving centre of trade in valuable pearl shell that was used for everything from high-quality buttons, buckles, hair-clasps and fancy pistol-grips, to timber cabinetwork inlay and the handles on elegant cutlery.

In the beginning of the pearl-shell industry Aborigines were employed (though not necessarily paid) to collect the shell; women in particular were 'blackbirded' into diving. Thursday Islanders gained a special reputation for their prowess at diving. But soon the pearling masters turned more to Asians, predominantly Japanese and Koepangers (Timorese), for divers and crew. The waterfront area ashore became known as Japtown, a vividly colourful tapestry of sorting sheds and providores; prostitutes and concubines; joss houses, gambling dens and grog shops.

Because of the importance of the divers to the industry, Broome was the first place in the country to be exempted from some of the provisions of the White Australia Policy. Descendants of marriages between diverse cultures have been spliced together over generations and are now proudly known as Broome Family People.

With the invention of plastic, pearl shell slowly lost its importance as an industry in the

North West, and the burning by the navy of the few pearling luggers that remained in the Second World War pretty much sealed its fate. Nevertheless, the town is still world famous for its 'tears of the moon', the cultured pearl industry now flourishes in underwater farms, and memories and reminders of the old pearl shell industry are alive and well, and all contribute to the attraction of Broome to tourists and travellers — along with a cosmopolitan and mellow population that encourages visitors to slip into 'Broome Time'.

One Broome Family Aboriginal elder, the grand-daughter of a white pearling master, is often to be found taking her ease along the foreshore. Anyone who takes the time and courtesy to listen to her will learn how her grandfather not only made a good income from pearling luggers but also branched out into another area of commerce. Every diver and crew member aboard every one of those 400 luggers, and most of the people ashore, ate rice as their staple food. How did they cook their rice? Over a wood fire, of course. It didn't take long before every stick of timber had been burned and every mangrove tree cut down along the foreshore. Her grandfather brought in firewood by sea from Carnarvon.

Today the mangroves have regrown, unchecked, and almost choke old Streeter's Jetty.

*

Broome is home port for the *Banana Mousskourri* VNW 3341, a James Wharram-designed cutter-rigged sloop, a wooden catamaran with aluminium mast and boom. A Wharram cat is unpretentious and very predictable. Based on a Polynesian concept of twin hulls and open deck between, Wharrams are popular among alternative lifestyle people because of their extreme simplicity of construction and performance.

*Banana Mousskourri* is no exception. Her 36-foot hulls are epoxied plywood and have a maximum beam of 5'8". Her slatted deck includes a small cockpit built out of half a fibreglass fuel tank washed up at high tide after an old game-fishing boat came to grief and broke up. Wheel steering is fitted in the cockpit. The overall beam across both hulls and deck is 19 feet.

The starboard hull contains the galley while the port hull contains navigation gear, radios, tools, spares and a fully operational marine head. Each hull contains two bunks, but the cockpit is just about double bed size, perfect for balmy tropical nights at anchor somewhere, under a mozzie net strung from the boom.

A cat is a logical choice of design for tropical waters because of its shallow draft and ability to move in light airs. However, every boat is a compromise in some respect and, because this boat has no fancy daggerboards to increase her draft, getting her to tack through the eye of the wind sometimes feels like trying to lead a camel through the eye of a needle.

As a concession to the rigours of the tidal patterns in this region, *Banana Mousskourri* also has a four-stroke outboard motor. Neap tides here have a greater range than spring tides down south, while springs here range from below the chart datum to above 9 metres or 30 feet. Because the length of time between tides varies little throughout the year, the result is strong tidal currents of 9 knots and more. The outboard is a safety back-up for those conditions.

*

As rough and tumble youngsters in rural districts, my siblings and cousins and I would walk out across the cold paddocks with a few dogs and a shovel, find a likely rabbit warren, and dig out a few rabbits. Hungry like most kids, we would then make a fire and cook a rabbit on the shovel. We learned that sandstone is not a suitable material out of which to build a fireplace — it explodes under heat!

Since then I have learned to improvise and make the best use of resources available, cooking in old neglected farmhouses with battered cast-iron wood stoves, where the firebricks had crumbled long ago, and outside, maybe a few herbs are still thriving in the derelict garden. Or on deer hunting trips in alpine country, with only a Swedish backpackers' spirit stove, where the liver of the quarry has such invigorating flavour. Or on duck-shooting trips when we return to camp exhausted from trudging around murky swamps infested with carp and tiger snakes, and the only equipment is an open fire and a cast-iron camp-oven, but that oven will cook an Irish stew untended for hours! Fishing trips and camping trips where the gear is just a primus stove burning kerosene under pressure, but the fish is so fresh and the paucity of equipment detracts nothing from the great pleasure of it all.

The transition from shore to ship's galley is easy, and it's worth repeating that a boat's galley does not need to be extravagantly appointed. On the van der Stadt trailer-sailer *Paean* the bench space was no larger than a sheet of A4 paper, but the scones and biscuits tasted just as good, and the size of the galley was effectively increased by hanging a marine barbecue off the stern rail. Barefoot rovers are inspired inventors, through necessity.

# Juringa's Sea Chanty

Give me the ocean! Salt wind on my face!
Hoist the tan yankee, and sheet home the main!

We'll set sail from Darwin: up anchors, a-weigh!
Out on the briny for many a day.

We'll watch Venus setting and sing to the moon,
Carousing with dugong and humming their tune.

Give me the ocean! Salt wind on my face!
Hoist the tan yankee, and sheet home the main!

We'll run down to Broome Town, past Buccaneer Rock,
And tie up at Streeter's, then walk the last block

Till we reach the old mangoes, full laden with fruit,
Then share (with the fruit bats) the plumping ripe loot.

Give thanks to the planter, who planted the seed,
Give thanks to the planter whatever her creed:

For it's chutney and pickle, to go with the bread,
And salted fresh tuna. We'll all be well fed!

Give me the ocean! Salt wind on my face!
Hoist the tan yankee and splice the mainbrace!

We'll pick up the trade winds and slacken the main,
Break out the spinney, then crack on again.

We'll follow the Horners across the high seas
And reach Valparaiso with consummate ease.

Oh! Give me the ocean! Salt wind on my face!
Hoist the tan yankee and sheet home the main!

This sea chanty I wrote for *Juringa* contains a few things that might need explaining. A chanty (from the French *chanson*) is a song sung to keep the crew working in time together, while hoisting the sails or hauling up the anchor, for instance. Cruising sails are often tan in colour to reduce glare on the eyes. A 'yankee' is a particular cut of jib, or headsail, on a cutter-rigged vessel. 'Sheet home the main' is the equivalent to saying put your foot on the accelerator in a car. 'Splice the mainbrace' is saying it's time for a drink. The spinney is the spinnaker, the largest sail. A Horner is a sailor who has rounded Cape Horn, and Valparaiso was the port where Horners congregated in the old days of sail, before the Panama Canal was built. To 'crack on again' is the old term for setting a cracking pace, going at top speed.

# Roving Profile: a family history

Both friends and strangers alike often ask two questions of me: how is it that I choose to spend so much time taking up the advice of the water-rat in *The Wind in the Willows*: '... there is nothing — absolutely nothing — half so much worth doing as simply messing about in boats,' and: where do the *Barefoot Roving* recipes come from? The answers to both questions are found in my family background.

It's all in my blood, the blood of Old Australians, descended from convicts, pioneers, whalers and nomads.

The Australian history of my father's family begins with Tom Scott, who set out from Scotland in 1820 to settle in Cape Town. When the *Skelton*, a ship of 260 tons, reached Africa she was quarantined 'without pratique' (no one was allowed ashore) because children on board had had measles. Earlier contact with measles had devastated the native African population. Tom remained on board for the next port of call, Hobart in the colony of Van Diemen's Land.

The journey aboard the *Skelton* lasted from 10 June to 28 November 1820, during which time Tom kept a tiny journal detailing life on board. His spidery copperplate handwriting records vivid details of daily life such as the sight of the shameless English coastal windmills still turning on the Sabbath, and that within just days of weighing anchor 'the goat belonging to Major McLeod had a young kid.' I wondered why anyone would want to include a heavily pregnant goat among their goods and chattels, but the journal goes on to reveal that the Major's wife was nearly ready for her own confinement, so the goat was probably a stand-by in case she did not survive childbirth or was otherwise unable to nurse the infant. During a gale and rough seas off Portugal on the night of 15 July, Mrs McLeod was safely delivered of a baby son.

Tom, aged twenty, was educated as a draftsman and surveyor. His journal entries mention that he often ruled and 'wrought' the captain's journal, and he records in his own pages the latitude and longitude, making it possible for today's reader to work out distances run.

His entries include folklore such as the entry for 15 August 1820, fifty-eight days out of Leith Roads, Scotland:

*Made the pudding for dinner today — and after dinner took in a pair of white trousers in the legs which were too wide before.*

*Bathing at night is not good for a person's constitution as it helps to check the perspiration which is essentially requisite in order to keep your health in this climate and on sea —*

*The Sea Air on the contrary is good for a man; whereas the land dews and night air is very prejudicial to the health. To get wet with sea water produces no ill effects whereas all the sailors dread rain water.*

The entry two days later gives the noonday sextant sight as 4°28'N, in other words very close to the equator. So it's easy to imagine him on deck with the crew in the lazy days and light airs of the tropics, learning from some garrulous sailor how to thread a needle and sew trousers.

His pen logs a colourful picture of other passengers and crew, conflicts of personalities, and the stress of living at close quarters on a long voyage travelling 'steerage' (or second class) with twenty-two men, eight women and twenty children passengers in the one hold. The first class cabin passengers numbered ten men, eleven women and twelve children, including the infant born under way. He mentions the merriment of a fiddler and dancing alongside reflections on the responsibilities of a young man set loose from the dour discipline and strict moral upbringing of a conservative Scottish home.

The entry for 3 July, fourteen days out of Leith, reads as follows:

*We had a strong meeting in the steerage about a partition to be sent to the Captain for a redress of grievance about getting bad butter and having to wash our own dishes. Given better butter and the crew has to wash the dishes.*

*Two of the boys on the forecastle had a shaking at one another and of them the least one cries 'come let alone or I'll sing out!' 'What will you sing out' cried the other. 'Murder in Irish,' cried he!*

And on Saturday 16 September:

*Strong wind all day with heavy rains S. Lat 30˚ 5' Long 14 ˚ W*
*The cook having lost 5 or 6 pairs of breeches overboard he got a piece of canvas from Mrs. Reedman's bed. She came down and fell a crying because the 2nd Mate had stripped off the rest. The 1st Mate came down and ordered another sail to be put up — and swore most terribly at the 2nd Mate. The carpenter said he had sailed 18 years & never had been in a ship where there was so much roguery.*

On Monday 23 October Tom spells out the rations:

*Very bad boiling tea today as the Cook forgot to boil us our pease soup*
*We get allowed by the Captain:*
*In the mornings — Porridge one morning and boiled rice the other*
*With a pound of raw sugar each weekly*
*1 lb of Sugar per week*
*1 lb of Flour and another of Rice do.*

*To make puddings for dinner;*
*with suet and raisins to mix it — half an English pint of Gin or Rum daily equal to*
*a Scotch gill or a quarter of a Mutchkin*
*1 lb of biscuit — 1 lb of Beef or 1 lb of Pork*
*& the dinner must serve for supper.*

Tom mentions a letter to his mother, posted aboard the *Lusitania* from Cape Town bound for London. Perhaps he was homesick and miserable by then, certainly he had been ill. His supply of tea had run out, and he was probably drinking contaminated water without boiling it first.

*

Like a cat, Tom fell on his feet in Hobart Town, where he was given the lucrative and interesting job of Assistant Surveyor General for the colony, for which he was paid in grants of land instead of money. He did a great deal of exploration work, much of it by sea, and drew the first detailed chart of the entire coast of the island. One hundred and fifty years after his arrival in Hobart, when my father donated Tom's journal to the library in Sydney, the library gave my father a copy of the chart. It hangs on my wall today, an eloquent link to my past and a great source of inspiration.

At the age of thirty-six, very wealthy and revealed by his portrait to be balding and rather tending to a portly physique, Thomas Scott returned to Scotland and married Anne Reid, aged just seventeen, a highland lassie, and daughter of the former Sheriff of London. Some of Anne's recipes are included in these pages.

Tom brought Anne back to Tasmania and built a home for her on the property which he named Cocked Hat Hill. For a navigator this name is synonymous with 'Mistake Hill'. (If you don't understand the association, it is explained in the recipe for cocked hat biscuits.) Records of wool sales show that for many years the highest price for the finest merino wool was paid by the

Japanese Imperial Household for fleece grown at Cocked Hat Hill.

Tom and Anne's descendants include their grandson James, my father's uncle, an original and courageous barefoot rover who ran away to Tonga and married a Tongan islander. Such behaviour was considered scandalous in those days.

James's brother was my grandfather Walter: a surveyor, bushman and explorer. Scott's Peak near Lake Pedder in Tasmania is named after him. Walter was also a keen sailor, racing the sleek Huon pine gaff-rigged cutter *Clutha* and roving the Tasmanian coast. His favourite destination was Port Davey — windswept, isolated and untamed, it was accessible only by sea.

*Clutha* measured 42 feet on deck, including bowsprit and counter stern, but only 21 feet on the waterline, and carried sails of jap silk. Walter sailed her to Launceston to race in the regatta on the Tamar River. There, the fresh water in the river meant she floated lower and therefore had a longer waterline length. Not to be accused of trying to cheat the race rules and receive an unfair advantage, Walter ran a wire from stem to stern and tweaked her up until the waterline length was again 21 feet. Only Tasmanian Huon pine would allow such drastic measures!

Walter's son, my father Arthur, was born in 1902 and grew up in Hobart where the back garden gate opened onto the Derwent River. When he lost his first milk-tooth at the age of six, his father taught him to swim by pushing him into the water off the little jetty outside the gate. His mother insisted all her sons sleep on the balcony, summer and winter, to 'toughen them up.' The balcony caught the full force of the southerly wind blowing up from Antarctica.

As a child, Arthur often spent weekends and school holidays aboard *Clutha* and knew intimately every bay and anchorage on the east coast, and every Bass Strait island. He knew by sight all the massive square-rigged windjammers that sailed past the garden gate to the docks in Hobart in the early 1900s. These ships carried apples from Tasmania and wheat and wool from the mainland around Cape Horn to the markets of Europe. Ships like the 3000-ton barque *Parma*, whose masts, towering 200 feet high, held aloft as many as twenty-eight sails: eighteen bent to the yards of the foremast, mainmast and mizzenmast; another two on the aft mast or jigger; and eight jibs and staysails.

When Arthur was about fourteen, he and his brothers and two friends set off on a bicycle tour of the countryside. As was traditional, they carried a tuckerbag full of oatmeal. After several days of a diet of oatmeal, and possibly the odd scrumpy apple, they called in at Bentleigh, the country estate of Arthur's prestigious uncle, the Honourable Cyril Cameron. Uncle Cyril was the member of parliament whose casting-vote decided whether the new federated nation's capital would be Melbourne, Sydney or the bush. The boys were eagerly looking forward to a hot dinner of roast beef and Yorkshire pudding, apple pie and custard. But the butler told them the master was not at home and had left no instructions about any scruffy boys on pushbikes. They were given permission to bunk down in the woolshed, and it was back to the oatmeal.

Next morning the boys left early, and Arthur left a note for his uncle, for which he remained in trouble for many a long day. The note read: 'If we had some ham, we'd have some ham and eggs, if we had some eggs.'

Uncle Cyril himself might be considered something of an eccentric. Bentleigh was a typical Tasmanian home of solid sandstone with gracious Georgian proportions. However, Cyril had added an extra room, built of timber, behind the main house. All meals were served in this room, the table elegantly set with embroidered table cloths, linen napkins, fresh flowers, crystal wine glasses, solid silver cutlery, and — beside the master's place — a loaded pistol. Whenever the master caught sight of a fly in the dining room he would fire at it, and the timber walls and ceiling were peppered with bullet holes.

Continuing the tradition of survey work and exploration my father Arthur, great-grandson of Tom, had the task of surveying the Arthur River on the west coast of Tasmania. The year was 1925 and my father told the story of how the ship carried them north from Hobart up the west coast. The bosun rowed the little party of five ashore from the ship at the entrance to the river, laughing and saying he'd be back in four months to collect them, if there were any of them left! That stretch of river is one of the very wildest and most remote there is. My father said he learned to understand the myth of how west-coasters 'walked across the top of the forest' to get to town. The westerly winds blow so hard and so relentlessly and the forest is so dense that the only way to make headway is to walk up a tree trunk that is bent to the power of the wind, then step onto the next beside and so make progress.

Arthur spoke also of finding the tracks of the five-toed thylacine around their camp, and to his dying day he believed those ancient creatures, thought to be extinct, could still be surviving along the Arthur River. Who knows?

Another barefoot rover of my father's generation was his cousin Con, who ran away to the Solomon Islands, and was dubbed King Con by a derisive press of the day. Con lived out his days in island contentment, no doubt leaving a wealth of descendants to carry on the tradition, and returned to the mainland only very late in life with failing health.

*

My mother's father's family also arrived in Australia by mistake. My mother's great-grandfather was Tom Burbury of Coventry, England, who, through a miscarriage of justice, was sentenced to be hanged. At the petition of his fellow locals, led by the church minister, the death sentence was commuted to transportation to Hobart Town aboard the *York* in 1832. Tom's wife Mary, whose father was the inn-keeper at the White Swan in Coventry, followed Tom to the end of the earth as a free settler. Letters written 'home' by Tom and Mary reveal some interesting details of their circumstances and it is easy to picture animated discussion over the letters among the locals enjoying a quiet glass of ale at the White Swan.

Mary was no whingeing Pom. Having survived the voyage to the colony with her two-year-old daughter Caroline, she next had to find her way to Anstey Barton, the farm where Tom had been assigned as a labourer.

To her family in England she wrote:

*I reached Hobart Town on the 12th of February, and found my husband was living about 50 miles up the country, at a place called Anstey Barton; as there are no coaches here, I agreed with a man who carries passengers and luggage, to take me up the country, for which he charged five pounds. We are living in a hut in the bush (or wood), which is very lonesome, being two miles from the nearest house, and that is the master's. Since I have joined my husband, he is allowed double rations; he has no wages, but gets a few shillings by hunting kangaroos when away from his sheep; the skins fetch from 3d to 6d a piece … [H]e is on rations, that is, 12lb of flour, 14lb of meat, 2lb of sugar, 4oz of tea, and 2oz of tobacco, per week; 4 shirts, 2 jackets, 2 waistcoats, and 2 pair of trousers a year, and what boots he requires. Many free labouring men are out of work at this time, but wages are higher here than in England; wearing apparel is about double the price it is at home. Flour is 2/- per stone; meat 5d per lb; tea has been very scarce, and lately as high as 5/- per lb. I never saw such tea drinkers in my life as people here, for they will put on the kettle, with two or three ounces of tea, and the sugar in it, and boil it all together; they then dip it out with a pot, and will see it out before they leave it, and this they will do three times a day. Better natured people to a stranger cannot be, for I have met with the kindest treatment from them, both where I am now living and at Hobart Town. A person used to the country might travel a hundred miles without a penny in his pocket, as he will never pass a hut without being asked to eat and drink, and to lodge if he chooses. This is a fine, healthy country, and very fertile; and though it is now the middle of winter, I have never seen ice or snow upon the ground, since I have been here. The mornings are cold, but the sun has as much power in the middle of the day now, as it has in England in May. Parrots fly about our hut as thick as house sparrows with you.*

In 1839 Tom Burbury was pardoned, a rare thing in those days, but he and Mary decided not to return to England. An important distinction between emancipated convicts (ticket of leave men) and those given a free pardon is that the former, though released from custody, were not permitted to return to the 'mother country'. With a free pardon Tom and Mary were free to return to Coventry, and certainly could well have afforded to do so, yet they never left Australia.

It is probably fair to say that the commonsense food management recorded in this book comes mostly from the Burburys. While Tom was a convict and not permitted to handle money, Mary, as a free settler, was able to set up a butcher's shop in Oatlands. With scant refrigeration they slaughtered on Mondays, and what was left by Friday they offered to the poor, free of charge. Together they prospered and became landowners, woolgrowers and graziers of the district.

The next generation remained on the land and included my mother's grandfather William. William and his wife Christiana raised thirteen children at Inglewood. Their eight sons, together with a few cousins from neighbouring properties, fielded their own cricket team in district matches. The 'farmstead' behind the rambling homestead was a grassed area the size of a cricket oval. On it was laid a cricket pitch of woven coir matting. District matches were a popular community affair involving elaborate picnic lunches and 'teas', and the luscious pies and pastries, cherry tarts, cream cakes and ginger beer were, of course, all homemade from homegrown produce.

Christiana's daughter-in-law Min continued the traditions of household management at Inglewood in the next generation. Another daughter-in-law, my grandmother Elsie Burbury, lived on the adjoining property, Fonthill. Gentle, patient, loving, and devoted, Elsie brought up seven children in a harmonious marriage. Like Min and Christiana, she did all the cooking, supervised the making of butter and cheese, and managed the preserving of jams, juices, sauces and pickles.

Fonthill had a stone staircase, and halfway up the stairs was a special room, cool and dark, called the stillroom, where preserves and ginger beer were stored. Bundles of dried herbs hung from the rafters, and crocks of pickled cucumbers and pickled onions, and whole regiments of jars of jams and preserved fruit and bottles of tomato sauce lined the silent shelves, for use in the following winter season.

My grandfather Sydney, Elsie's husband, was a man who lived by his religious principles. One winter's day a shepherd (as the stockmen are still called in Tasmania) arrived at the kitchen door with a message from Sydney. The shepherd was wet and cold and Elsie told him to sit by the fire while she attended to the details of the message. The children, including my mother Lilian, were all aged under ten. One of them handed the shepherd their father's newspaper to read while he waited. Shortly, the children collapsed into gales of giggles when they saw that the man held the paper as though reading it, except that it was upside-down. They couldn't decide whether he was so clever he could read it anyway, or if he was an adult who couldn't read. Elsie did not want to embarrass the man, and when Sydney came home he decided it was unfair that his brood alone should have the privilege of a governess, and he opened a school on the sheep station so that the children of the shepherds and his children could learn together.

Letters Elsie and Syd wrote to my mother when she was married with children of her own reveal the close bond of their marriage, and a close connection to the land and the vagaries of the seasons. Syd, well into his sixties, a crusty old wool-grower and grazier still tending ewes and marking lambs, wrote in August 1934:

*I don't often write to you, but for a change to show you I have not altogether forgotten you I will — Mother as you know has been with Jean for a long time now, & you can imagine how I miss her, she grows dearer & dearer to me as the years roll on, and I do miss her so much. Of course under the circumstances, I am quite prepared to put up with it all, as I know what her presence at Jean's bedside means ...*

Very late in life Syd bought the second motor car sold in Tasmania, after having lived and worked with horses all his life. Mother said he learned to start the car with the crank-handle and to change gears from first up to second, and on up to third, which was top gear. However, he never really got the hang of changing down, and when the engine began to labour on a hill, he would lean forward and urge the horses on!

My mother, Lilian Burbury, grew up at Fonthill. To collect the mail the children rode their horses nine miles. Lilian must have been an accomplished horse-rider from an early age. During the First World War, when she was aged between eight and twelve, government officials moved through the district requisitioning the best horses to provide mounts for the Australian Light Horse Infantry. Lilian's horse Swordsman was among those requisitioned.

The officials promised Lilian her mount would be returned after the war. But Old Australians know that the Australian Light Horse Infantrymen are famous for their defiance of one particular order. After four years with their mounts in the harsh conditions of the battlefields of the Middle East, sharing their water and food, sleeping beside their horses and depending on them for the safety of their lives, the order came at the end of the war that every man must shoot his horse. The men refused, and in the end, every man shot the next man's horse.

Lilian never forgave the authorities for failing to meet their end of the bargain and thereafter held the greatest contempt for all government officialdom and regulation. No politician could ever buy her vote.

Fiercely independent, and with a great respect for life, Lilian lived through two world wars and the Great Depression. Those were hard times, indeed. Nothing was ever wasted in the household, food was treated with reverent respect, and grace was said before every meal. She too bottled hundreds of jars of fruit, juices and jam; pickled walnuts, beetroot and onions; baked bread and made chutney, all of those things that can make home such a welcoming place.

*

Between them, my parents taught me to respect food, which is to respect life; to be content without great material wealth, not forever seeking more; to value wild places, silence, patience and self-reliance, and to grasp the perspective of the big picture, in which my self is infinitely small.

# The Barefoot Galley
## equipment, stores & the cook's log

'Presentation is everything!' declares Tim Jones with a hearty laugh, as another spicy concoction is handed up out of the galley on *Juringa*. By this he means the presentation of good food in a stunning location of natural beauty and fresh air beats by a country mile any stilted arrangements offered on half-empty plates in fancy restaurants.

I sailed on the *Juringa* with Dave Legge and Tim, and its galley was really the best I have worked in. Everything was within arm's reach from a seat opposite the stove; portholes gave plenty of daylight and fresh air to the cook and extra bench surfaces telescoped out from under the stove. A freshwater pump was installed beside the stove, but there was no actual sink — just a small bowl. Washing up was done on deck using a bucket of sea water. Of course there was no fridge, but nets were strung from various points to hold fruit and vegetables.

The stability of a cat on the water certainly makes life easier for the cook under way, and the tropical climate means almost all meals are eaten on deck. A small hole cut through the deck outside the galley hatch meant biodegradable scraps could be 'posted' through to the water beneath. After dark the warm soft light of a cuddy lamp shone from a hook on the cabin roof above the bench. The barefoot roving enjoyment of that galley included the silence and the soft sound of lapping water at a sheltered anchorage. No noisy electric cooking appliances, no generator thumping, no engine running to keep the fridge cold, just peace and contentment.

Food goes down better in a state of harmony and peace of mind. And on a cruising boat, harmony and peace of mind pivot around clear foresight where food is concerned. Compared even to the contemporary townhouse's chic kitchenette, a cruising yacht's galley is a tiny work-space.

Planning and organisation are essential, and the essence of good planning lies in simplicity and self-reliance.

Confidence in self-reliance builds with practice, as galley cooking evolves into an art. Just a little practice soon knits up 'the ravelled sleave of care' and turns all the cook's worries into neat solutions. Cooking and food preparation, thank goodness, placidly encompass a huge margin of error.

*

Most boat-owners will speak of the live presence of a boat's personality. Equally, the galley on every boat seems to me to convey a distinct presence of its own. The galley on the *Banana Mousskourri* is in the starboard hull. There is a saltwater hand-pump at the sink, as well as a freshwater pump. A single-burner pressure kero stove straddles the bench. The galley, like that on the *Juringa*, is a totally relaxed, refrigeration-free, worry-free zone and contains only the simplest cookware. The Barefoot Banana Safe (see page 249) is out on deck, hanging in the shade to catch the cooling breeze.

*

How long ago was the first hearth bread kneaded and baked? Did that cook rely on a thermostatically controlled, stainless steel self-cleaning electric bread machine? Things don't need to be high-tech sophisticated to prove reliable and trustworthy. Uncomplicated, hand-operated tools like wooden spoons, graters, whisks, mincers, and pestle and mortar have proven their worth and reliability over countless generations.

A two-frame cartoon of Hagar the Horrible by Dik Browne first shows Hagar's best mate ruminating over the fact that Hagar could have saved the food and drink in a shipwreck. The second frame reveals that Hagar chose instead to save his golf clubs, explaining 'but these are old friends!' I feel the same nostalgia for my cooking utensils; they too are old friends, respected and cherished. It's not just idiosyncrasy: the familiarity of well-used cooking utensils seems to endow them each with a personality. And their diversity is part of what turns cooking into an art.

# Utensils

Some of my most precious cookware, such as my cast-iron girdle, my bakelite-handled double-boiler, my hand beater, hand mincer and hachinette, are available only in pricey Antique Shoppes these days. I feel like a bit of an antique myself, but it's well worth scouring flea markets to find the most reliable utensils, the ones that become old friends.

A **pressure kero stove** is my choice aboard a boat. On a pressure kero stove, if the flame blows out the fuel stops flowing. And kero is a 'third world' fuel, available in the kinds of places I like to visit. In places like Kalumburu in the Kimberley, metho for metho stoves is difficult to find, not to mention that it's as pricey as French brandy in the attempt to deter its use as an object of substance abuse.

My oven, a **Dutch oven** sitting atop the pressure kero burner, contains no thermostat, let alone a thermostatically controlled fuel supply. The oven is made of cast alloy and has a domed lid. I believe the domed shape of the lid helps the heat to circulate efficiently inside the oven. Cast alloy and cast iron seem to conduct heat more efficiently than stainless steel.

Stamped into the bottom of my Dutch oven is the now rare inscription: 'Made in Australia', which probably makes it a collector's item at thirty years of age.

A **pressure cooker** is almost essential in a barefoot galley, the time it saves paling into insignificance beside the fuel it saves. My second-hand SEB cooker, looking like it's old enough to have been left over from the Light Horse Infantry, has the advantage of two small handles, which take less space than one large handle in a small galley. Replacement parts for gaskets, handles, weights and so forth are readily available from city stores.

Frying pans and griddles both have a handle sticking out on the same plane as the cooking-surface of the pan. Such a handle can be a danger in a cramped galley. A piece of equipment well-known to our forebears was the **girdle** (pronounced g*eer*dle), a cast-iron disc with a raised rim and a handle over the top like a bucket handle. A girdle was often suspended over the hearth, the handle forged with a kink so that it would balance in the exact middle. A girdle makes toast, crumpets and toasted sandwiches, and bakes flatbread, biscuits, pikelets, pancakes and drop-scones (made from scone dough with the addition of an egg, which makes a batter just able to drop from the spoon). A girdle also stows away easily because the handle folds down neatly.

A **double boiler** is a small pot suspended inside a larger pot. The purpose of the suspension is to prevent the bottom of the small pot coming into direct contact with the fire. Instead, it touches only the boiling water inside the larger pot, which all 'boils down' to the wonderful fact that your sauce doesn't burn, and your grain doesn't need stirring while it cooks.

A **hachinette** is a small wooden bowl paired with a special cutting blade shaped to match the inside profile of the bowl. As you chop herbs, or walnuts, or ginger, for instance, the pieces drop back into the bottom of the bowl.

A **whistling kettle** helps conserve fuel.

Another old favourite among my galley equipment is a metal **measuring cone**. Most often I measure ingredients by volume, not weight. Inside the cone are increments of measurement for flour, sugar, semolina, ground almonds, rolled oats and so forth, indicating the corresponding weight.

# Stores & the cook's log

For self-reliance in remote areas, staples like flour, sugar, salt, milk powder, beans, grains, and so forth must be carried in bulk. (Some other very useful staples are mentioned in 'Galley Pearls' which follows.) Bulk supplies can be stowed in a relatively inaccessible place if small quantities are decanted for easier use in the galley, a fortnight's supply at a time, for instance.

Good galley management on a cruising boat includes a log of stores loaded, stowed and used, including details of what is stowed where. Whether your log is kept 'with a thumbnail dipped in tar' or on a fancy PC spreadsheet, it will serve no worthwhile purpose unless you keep it up to date. Running comments on spoilage or accessibility or crew preferences might make the whole job easier next time.

The cook's log can be just as important as the skipper's log when it comes to remembering exactly which island had that little stand of quandong, which reef gave us the fattest, tastiest trepang, which anchorage gave the most easily accessible fresh water in the dry season, and where those bird's eye chilies were growing in rank profusion.

The cook's log also keeps track of the quantity of fresh water stowed on board, and how often stores were supplemented by fresh seafood. It should also keep track of just how many people have been fed, for if the delicious aroma of freshly baked bread and cakes wafts over to neighbouring yachts anchored in the same bay, you'll find you have lots of visitors and extra mouths to feed.

# Galley Pearls

Here I wish to offer a few pearls of wisdom pertaining to the galley, gathered the hard way, though not quite so hard as the way the hard-hat divers of yesteryear gathered their pearls from the sea floor. Those men had lead boots and a copper helmet, and their best mate on deck tirelessly turning, by hand, the air-pump which forced air down the hose to the helmet.

**Alcohol** evaporates at a temperature far lower than that at which water evaporates. So if you wish your brandy sauce or your lamb's wool drink to retain its alcohol, make sure it has cooled down sufficiently to avoid evaporation before you slosh in the grog.

**Baking powder** Run out? Make your own: 180g (6oz) cornflour, rice flour or arrowroot; 120g (4oz) bicarbonate of soda (baking soda); 120g (4oz) cream of tartar; 120g (4oz) tartaric acid. Shake it all together well, in a plastic bag or a jar, and store it as dry as possible. The humidity destroys its power.

**Batter** By far the easiest, lightest, crispiest batter for pieces of fried fish, or hard cheese, or pineapple fritters is simply the following: beat together cold water and SR flour until you have a batter of light coating consistency. An added pinch of salt and a pinch of citric acid brings out the flavour of fish. Coat the pieces first with plain flour, then dip them in the batter, then straight into hot clean fat or oil.

**Bay leaves** Usually used as a flavouring for baked custards or fish dishes, bay leaves are also a strong deterrent for weevils. The dried leaves of the yam bean vine, which contain rotenone, act as a deterrent for cockroaches.

**Butter** means ghee in the tropics. Butter is essential in barefoot stores, but it must be tinned and is sold as ghee, or clarified butter. North of 18°S, ghee is already liquid when you open the tin, so a recipe for pastry saying 'rub in the butter' means stir in the ghee with a knife.

**Citric acid** in powdered form is a very useful substitute for lime juice or vinegar. It is readily available in grocery stores, usually out of sight among the baking powders and spices. For a rule-of-thumb measure, half a teaspoon of citric acid equals 2 tablespoons of lime juice or vinegar. Citric acid has the best flavour, but if you run out, tartaric acid will do, and salicylic acid (aspirin left exposed to the air overnight) is a useful substitute — in fact they're all essential galley stores.

**Coconuts** Green coconuts contain 'milk' and a coating of flesh the consistency of jelly. This is all delicious to eat and drink but not suitable for making coconut cream. To determine the ripeness of a nut the cook needs to learn the skill of shaking the nut and listening to the amount of liquid milk sloshing around inside. Ripening takes months, but the riper the nut becomes the less sound is heard as the liquid transforms into a seed, the nut, intended by nature to grow into another tree.

**Coconut cream** is made from the mature solid flesh lining the shell. After the flesh has been grated it needs to be wrung out through muslin cloth or through a piece of the fibre which grows around the base of a coconut tree and looks like burlap. Freeze-dried coconut powder can be reconstituted as either thin milk or thick cream. The amount of water used is all that makes the difference.

**Condensed milk** If a recipe calls for sweetened condensed milk and you have none, make your own this way: dissolve 1¾ cups of white sugar into 1 cup of boiling water; when cooled, add 2 cups of full cream milk powder.

**Cornflour or arrowroot?** Cornflour contains all starch and no protein. For the cook this means that a very little cornflour will thicken soup or stew. This is the method traditionally used to thicken stir-fry, but cornflour must boil to do this, and it does not take up the fat as it thickens a dish, so the fat remains on the surface. Arrowroot will also thicken things but, unlike cornflour, it does not need to boil to do so. It also has far more food value than cornflour, and it will absorb the fat.

The easiest way to thicken the contents of the pressure cooker after all is cooked and the pressure is reduced, is to stir in some arrowroot which has been mixed with water into a thin paste. It will still be hot enough for the thickening to happen without boiling.

**Egg substitutes** A recipe for a substitute for fresh eggs, offered in the Royal Flying Doctor *Mantle of Safety Cookbook 2*, advises the cook to pulp the flesh of two oranges and mix it with a cup of vinegar and a tablespoon of sugar. After standing overnight, it is placed in a closed jar in a pan of boiling water for 10 minutes. One tablespoon of the mix takes the place of one egg.

In recipes such as Fish Toes, which use egg to bind the ingredients together, a last resort substitute is 2 teaspoons of arrowroot per egg.

In recipes for cakes and fancy breads, vinegar (a dessertspoonful per egg) will help the 'glomming' of the flour and liquid. (Glomming is the baker's term for the transformation of flour and water into dough.)

**Emulsion** Mustard is well-known as an emulsifying agent to persuade oil and vinegar to blend together to form a salad dressing or a dressing for cold seafood. Less well-known for the same task is honey — real honey, straight from the hive, not pasteurised, not blended with caramel syrup, and not from bees fed antibiotics.

**Fat** The medium in which you fry something has a direct bearing on the flavour of the finished article. Different fats have distinct flavours and dirty fat is a disaster. To clean fat that has become overburdened with food particles, such as breadcrumbs or fragments of batter, boil up the fat in a quantity of water twice its volume. When this cools it separates; the now-clean fat rises to the surface and the now-dirty water settles to the bottom.

**Fish sauce** I don't generally like to tout brands, but when it comes to fish sauce in a recipe, Squid Brand Fish Sauce (Nuoc Mam) is miles and away the best. You can find it in Asian groceries and on supermarket shelves, which is just as well, since between Broome and Cairns across the top — a distance further than across Europe — there's probably only Darwin big enough to have an Asian grocery.

**Fire** is a good galley servant and a bad master. Be vigilant. Totally avoid hazards like hanging curtains near a galley flame. Avoid the build-up of vaporised cooking oil, which clings as a coating of flammable oil over surfaces such as bench tops and locker doors. When cooking, have a wet towel within easy reach, for smothering out-of-control flame.

**Ghee** See butter.

# Home drying
Biltong (jerky), dried meat or dried fish, or even dried fruit leathers are not easy food preservation systems to manage in the tropics. Humidity levels and spoilers have the upper hand too much of the time. Tomatoes are the exception. Small tomatoes, well ripened, can be cross-sectioned in half, dusted with salt (rock salt must be used) and sugar, then dried in direct sunlight. They shrivel and turn leathery, and are then ready to be stored in jars, submerged in olive oil. The inclusion of herbs such as thyme in the oil will not only improve the flavour but will add to the preservation.

# Kambotscha
– the 'Tea Beast' – is well worth brewing on board. Try whatever it takes to find someone willing to share the culture with you. See page 228 for details.

# Salt
, in my galley, means cooking salt or rock salt, definitely not table salt. Table salt contains 'something special' to make it run.

# Sippets
(also known by their French name, croutons) are small cubes of bread – stale bread is fine – fried quickly in butter or bacon fat until crisp. They are served hot, usually from a separate bowl, and sprinkled onto the surface of a bowl of hot soup where they float like small boats. Although unfashionable by today's dietary standards, they remain undeniably delicious.

# Smoking
The term smoking applies to two different treatments of meat, fish and some cheeses: hot smoking and cold smoking. Cold smoking is an elaborate and time-consuming method of preserving meat or fish (e.g. ham, red salmon) demanding cold temperatures, so it is highly unsuitable for a barefoot rover in tropical latitudes. Hot smoking, on the other hand, as in the recipe for smoked fish, is not done to preserve the meat or fish (though as in any cooking process, it kills most bacteria as it cooks the flesh), but for the appetising flavour it imparts.

**SR flour** Run out of SR flour? Make your own: into 5 cups of plain flour mix and distribute well 2 teaspoons of cream of tartar, 1 teaspoon of bicarbonate of soda, a pinch of sugar and a pinch of salt. Plain flour is usually 'soft' flour, suitable for cakes and pastry, but 'hard' flour for breadmaking may also be used.

**Sterilising powder**, available from home-brew supplies, is also essential food management equipment. Sterilise drink bottles and jam jars before re-using them to avoid unwanted yeasts and bacteria. Sterilise the containers (traditionally called 'breakers') used for replenishing the water supply carried on board. See also 'Food Safety in the Tropics'.

**Sugar** Yeasts, which can be nurtured to make leavening agents for bread, include in their vast family yeasts and moulds which become spoilers of foods, especially in the warmth and humidity of the tropics. To counter the enthusiasm of unwanted yeasts in any food, bear in mind that an excessive amount of sugar, such as is used in jams, shrinks yeast cells and prevents budding (reproduction). Excess salt has a similar effect, which is why corned beef is saturated in salt and why pickled pork and sea biscuits were the main diet of early seafarers.

**Tartaric acid** If you wish to clean the scale from the inside of an old kettle, two teaspoons of tartaric acid crystals boiling in one pint of water should lift it clear after a few minutes' boiling.

**Unsalted butter** Unsalted commercial butter is not merely butter without salt; it is matured, like cultured sour cream, and contributes towards successful cake-rising, and pastry lightness. If you have the luxury of unsalted butter among your stores, don't forget to compensate for its missing salt, or your finished dish will lack flavour.

# Water and cooking fuel

Sea-steading skills include dedicated and methodical conservation of resources. If you set out to make two cups of tea don't boil up six cups of water! Measure the water first and use a whistling kettle. And to conserve water in food preparation, stand a bowl inside the galley sink to act as a reservoir of rinsing water.

# Barefoot Recipes

PINDAN WATTLE
BROOME HONEY

# Preserves & Preserving

In days of old, Christmas ham was not made because it was Christmas: it was made in order to preserve the meat without refrigeration and without the technology of canning or freeze-drying. What we enjoy as 'flavour' in ham — the salt and smoke, sugar, molasses and cloves — was added for the purpose of preservation. Today we regard vinegar, mustard and dill seed as essential flavour in pickled gherkins. We tend to forget that their first purpose was that of preservation.

The following substances best known today for their flavour, are enjoying a revival of popularity among barefoot rovers for their powers of preservation:

| | |
|---|---|
| salt | sugar |
| ginger | citrus juice |
| vinegar | pepper |
| citric acid | garlic |
| cayenne | mustard |
| onion | chili |
| Jamaica pepper (allspice) | tea |
| dill | coriander |
| cinnamon | cloves |
| tamarind | honey (unrefined) |
| mace | |

Unrefined honey, by the way, was the only kind of honey you could come by in my great-grandmother's day — straight from the comb, not sterilised, not diluted with sugar syrup, and not from bees fed antibiotics. Luckily you can still find it today.

Old recipe books are consistently reliable as a source of information on preserves and preserving, simply because in the olden days preservation was the primary objective of the recipe. By sad comparison, today's recipes in glossy magazines, with living-colour, luscious photographs, seem more concerned with visual impact. For instance, a contemporary recipe for a jar of pickled tricoloured bell peppers is intended, by instruction, to be popped in the fridge. It could not be expected to last in the bilge of a tropical cruiser.

## Jams, chutneys, mustard & vinegar

Our trusty old Wharram catamaran, *Banana Mousskourri*, gets hauled out of the water every wet season to avoid cyclones and to enjoy some serious maintenance.

The wet season in Broome coincides with harvest in other areas, and in this time I put by stores of jams and pickles onshore, ready to stow aboard for the next venture. Some recipes, like those for tamarind chutney and dried apricot jam, are so simple they can be conjured together anywhere along a cruise.

# Template for jam making

For rule-of-thumb jam making, remember it is the sugar, spice and boiling that preserves the fruit as jam, while the pectin contributes most towards the set (the consistency of the jam). Citrus pips contain high concentrations of pectin, which can be extracted by a process of osmosis. Soak the pips overnight in enough water to cover them; drain, discard the pips and use the water for jam-making. Rosella seeds also contain a high concentration of pectin, and again, you can soak them overnight, strain them and use the water. Apple seeds contain arsenic. Early in the last century a little arsenic used to be a fashionable tonic. A few seeds would not contain enough to cause harm, but too much is fatal, so perhaps err on the side of caution.

As a basic rule of jam making stick to the following pattern:

Select fruit which is in good condition. Overripe and bad fruit makes bad jam (fancy that!). Chop or slice the fruit to speed up the cooking. Try to cut them to a uniform size so that they all need the same length of time to cook. Cook in a small quantity of water at just below boiling point. Juice will flow out of the cooking fruit.

Measure the volume of cooked fruit and juice and add an equal volume of sugar, or less if the pectin content is high.

Add 'flavouring' such as mace, cloves, nutmeg and cardamom.

Boil together the fruit, juice, sugar and spice for at least 10 minutes at a rollicking boil before storing in sterile jars and sealing down.

Remember, too-thin jam can be renamed ice-cream topping, or with a dash of vinegar it becomes piquant sauce.

## The pectin test

Put 2 teaspoons of methylated spirits into an egg cup and add 1 teaspoon of boiling liquid from the stewed fruit, before the sugar has been added. Allow this to remain quite still for two minutes. If the juice forms a thick jelly it contains enough pectin to 'set'. If it's too thin, powdered pectin can be added, but allow it to disperse well and blend evenly as it melts, before you dump in the sugar. If you have no powdered pectin but are still determined to have thick jam the solution is to boil the liquid until it reduces in volume.

Fowlers Vacola produce powdered pectin and are the respected authority on the subject of preserves. Their instructions on the packet of pectin read: 'as a rule-of-thumb guide for your favourite jam recipe, allow a 50g packet of Jamsetta to 1 kg prepared raw fruit. Simply cook fruit until soft, then add Jamsetta and warmed sugar, stirring until dissolved. Bring to the boil and boil vigorously for five minutes, stirring occasionally.'

# Dried Apricot Jam

250g dried apricots

4 cups cold water

1 teaspoon citric acid

4 cups sugar

Soak the dried fruit in the water overnight. Bring the fruit and soaking water to the boil and simmer gently for 12 to 15 minutes. Add the citric acid and the sugar, stirring until the sugar dissolves. Let it boil a further 15 minutes then seal in sterilised jars.

# Green Mango Chutney

Select green mangoes that are so immature that it is easy to cut through the core.

2$^1/_2$ kg green mangoes

4 cups vinegar

2$^1/_2$ kg white sugar

2 red chilies

garlic (optional)

250g raisins

250g ginger, fresh or sweet-preserved

1 tablespoon salt

2 tablespoons whole cloves

Peel the mangoes with a potato peeler. Cut the flesh into strips about 6 mm thick and 2 or 3 mm long. Bring vinegar and sugar to the boil, add other ingredients and cook until the mangoes are just translucent. Pack the fruit into jars and submerge under syrup.

# Quickest Chutney

1 tablespoon vinegar from a jar of pickled onions

3 tablespoons jam (plum or apricot)

1 tablespoon Worcestershire sauce

Blend the vinegar, jam and Worcestershire sauce; no further 'cooking' is necessary. If you remember the proportions, namely 1 : 3 : 1, you can extemporise on this, using soy sauce or chili sauce in place of Worcestershire, for instance, or chopped raisins and honey instead of jam.

# Rosella Chutney

From Hamish, who grows the best potatoes on Norfolk Island. Rosellas grow wild on the Dampier peninsula. It is the juicy calyx of the rosella fruit that is eaten.

$1\frac{1}{2}$ cups vinegar

4 cups brown sugar

1 teaspoon salt

4 cups ripe rosella calyx and 6 green seed pouches

$\frac{1}{2}$ cup raisins

1 clove garlic, 1 red chili and a thimble-sized piece of ginger
    chopped and mixed together

Boil the vinegar with the salt and sugar. Add the rosellas, seeds and raisins and cook at a rollicking boil until it is thick. Add the remaining ingredients and boil a further 10 minutes before bottling and sealing.

# Tamarind Chutney

$^1/_3$ cup tamarind pulp

$^3/_4$ cup dates

$^1/_2$ teaspoon chopped fresh ginger

1 fresh green chili, chopped

$^1/_2$ cup sugar (white or brown)

1 teaspoon salt

$1^1/_2$ teaspoons garam masala

$^1/_2$ teaspoon cayenne pepper

Soak the tamarind pulp in a cup of hot water for 1 hour. Soak the dates in half a cup of hot water for 1 hour. In a saucepan mix the dates, their soaking water, the ginger, chili and another cup of water, and simmer together for 15 minutes. Remove from the heat. Squeeze out all the pulp from the soaked tamarind, sieve it, reserve the puree, discard the fibre and stones.

Combine tamarind puree well with the date mixture; add salt, sugar and spice. Bring to a rollicking boil, stirring until the sugar has dissolved. Boil for 7 to 10 minutes.

# Mustard

Freshly made mustard is as easy as crushing mustard seed into powder and mixing it into a paste with cold water. Its characteristically pungent flavour does not develop until cold water is mixed with the powdered seed. This is the work of enzymes acting on certain elements called glucosides (sugars) and it needs time to develop fully, maybe ten minutes.

Bitterness rather than pungency will be the result if anything other than cold water is used to mix with the crushed seed. Recipes calling for cream, hot water, wine or vinegar to mix the mustard will therefore create a bitter condiment.

Dry powdered mustard seed is the simplest to use for freshly prepared oil and vinegar dressings where an emulsifying agent is needed, although 'made mustard' will do too.

In its whole spice form, mustard is the seed from three different plants of the cabbage family, known by their Latin names as *nigra* (black), *juncea* (brown), and *alba* (white). Nigra seed has the strongest condiment flavour, but is also the least successfully manipulated for commercial farming. Juncea seed is more tractable to commercial cropping but has a weaker flavour; it is often nicknamed 'black'. Alba has the least pungency, but the strongest power of preservation, discouraging bacterial spoilers and moulds.

For preservation, alba seed is the most appropriate for jars of pickled eggs or pickled bush lemons.

# Vinegar

Vinegar is possibly the most useful, versatile and eloquent ingredient in a barefoot galley. Its antiseptic properties counter spoilers in food and on utensils, it sharpens sauces and gravies, dressings and drinks, and is a major contributor to preservation without refrigeration. Unfortunately, most people have forgotten how to make it from scratch. The gooseberry vinegar below is a recipe from my great-great-grandmother's recipe book, dated 1836. The term 'toast and yest' means a slice of toasted bread spread with live bread-sour.

> *Gooseberry Vinegar: Boil spring water; and when cold, put to every three quarts a quart of bruised gooseberries in a large tub. Let them remain sixty hours, stirring often; then strain through a hair bag, and to each gallon of liquor add a pound of the coarsest sugar. Put it into a barrel, and a toast and yest. Mind that the cask be full, and set over a tub to work. Set the barrel in the sun. When it ceases to ferment, cover the bung hole with a piece of slate. The greater the quantity of sugar and fruit, the stronger the vinegar; and as this is particularly useful for pickles, it might be well to make it of double the strength for that purpose.*

Vinegar is best known as wine that's gone sour, but good vinegar is no hit and miss product. Good vinegar develops through the entirely natural process of the action of yeast working on any liquid containing sugar of any sort to ferment it and form alcohol. Once alcohol has been created two things can be controlled next. The fermented alcoholic liquid can be closely corked to the exclusion of air (for wine), or, 'spoilers' can be allowed to take over and oxidise the alcohol to acetic acid, simply by leaving it uncorked. The uncorked product becomes vinegar, and the flavour of the vinegar relates directly to the essence of the sweet liquid worked on in the first place — apple juice, pawpaw, grape juice or whatever. Good vinegar comes from good ingredients.

The slow patient process needed to make top quality vinegar requires a controlled temperature of 21°C, not feasible in the tropics without air-conditioning. You can however keep cider vinegar brewing, or make vinegar with the Tea Beast culture (see kambotscha). Otherwise be content to pay the price deserved for good quality vinegar.

Many vinegars are now on the market. For washing down benches and chopping-boards plain white vinegar is fine, but cooking and preserving deserve something more. I find the most versatile is cider vinegar, which allows me the added benefit of continuing to brew apple skins. Cider vinegar is also recognised as a folk medicine. I carry brown malt vinegar for pickled onions and for Auntie Min's Cake. It is the red wine vinegar that gives kalamata olives their special flavour. I find balsamic vinegar so intense in flavouring that it overpowers everything if not used very sparingly. For instance a salad dressing of oil and cider vinegar can be 50% vinegar, but with balsamic, you only need 10% vinegar or it is too overpowering.

If you buy vinegar, be selective. When the claim on the bottle is 'low acid content' this is another term for 'watered down'. If the purpose of your vinegar is preservation the acid strength must be high, at least 6 per cent. High price is not always a reflection of high value. Resist the temptation to pay large sums of money for average quality vinegar flavoured with lavish additions of tarragon, for instance. A good quality balsamic vinegar, such as from Cooper's Brewery in Leabrook, South Australia, costs about the same as cheap wine, but there the similarity ends. Cooper's balsamic has a rich, inspiring complexity of flavours, a sort of Bayeux tapestry for the taste buds, and worth every cent.

# Cider Vinegar

**apple peel**

**1 tablespoon vinegar (from a previous batch, or shop-bought)**

Cider vinegar can be kept on the brew in the galley. Save apple peel and pack it into a scrupulously clean glass jar, such as a 3.5 cup (750 ml) coffee jar with a glass lid. Add 1 tablespoon of mature vinegar and fill up the jar with water. Close it to exclude unwanted yeasts, and let it brew for several days. The longer you leave it the stronger it gets. It is important to use a lid on the jar, but not a metal one as metal is corroded by the acid in vinegar.

# Spiced Vinegar

To flavour the vinegar, take about half a cup of any vinegar (except balsamic, which already has a strong flavour) and heat it with your chosen spices, holding it just below boiling point for 3 minutes to infuse the flavours. Then top up with unboiled plain vinegar.

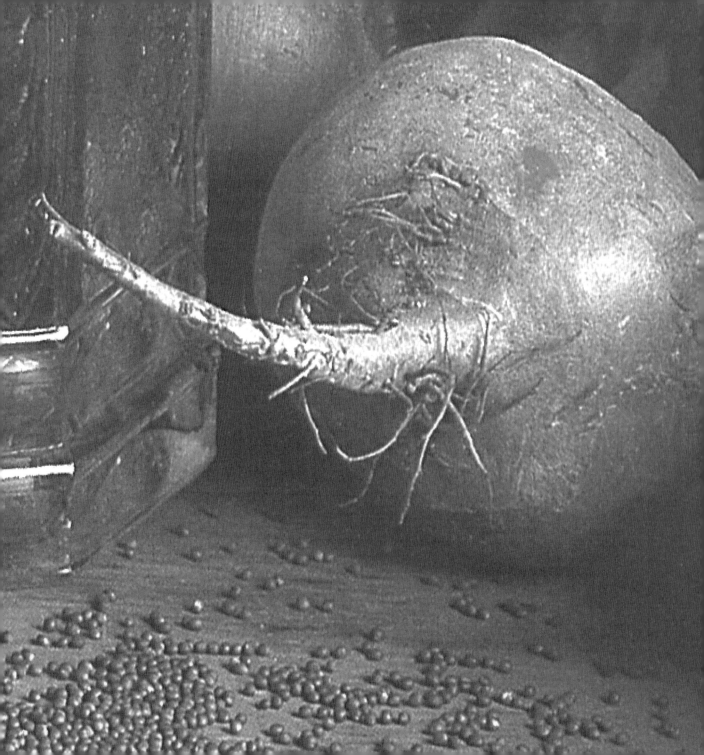

# Preserved Vegetables

## Beetroot

Homemade beetroot is the perfect foil for home salted fish.

> **beets**
> **spiced vinegar (mace, cloves and cardamom)**
> **sugar (to taste)**

Select beets of uniform size so that they all need a similar length of time to cook. Trim the leaves off the top of the plant but don't cut into the bulb, leave 10 mm of stem, and don't trim the roots, just wash them. Try to leave the skin of the bulb unpunctured. These precautions are not essential, but they help retain the juice in the bulb.

Put the beets in the pressure cooker with water reaching one quarter their height. Bring them up to pressure and cook for about 15 minutes or until tender. When cooled, slip the skins off and slice the beets into a jar with a plastic or glass lid.

Prepare a vinegar in which to submerge them, spiced with mace, cloves and cardamom and sweetened with sugar. Beets are ready to eat immediately, but improve with keeping.

When pickling anything in vinegar, remember that a metal lid may corrode in the acid of the vinegar. Glass coffee jars with plastic inserts in glass lids are perfect.

# Pickled Cabbage

Pickled cabbage is not the same as sauerkraut. Genuine sauerkraut is a ferment that needs a temperature lower than that north of 18°S. Real sauerkraut does not include vinegar. I prepare pickled cabbage in Broome in the wet season, ready to take away.

> **2 kg young red cabbage (or green)**
>
> **3 tablespoons cooking salt**
>
> **spiced vinegar (pimento and caraway seed)**

'First, catch your cabbage' — select a good quality young cabbage, preferably red. Its leaves should be so dense that it feels very heavy for its size. Shred it, as you would for coleslaw, discarding the core and the coarsest outer leaves. Pack the shredded leaves into a glass casserole dish in alternating layers of cabbage and cooking salt, ending with a top layer of salt.

A ratio of 3 level tablespoons of salt to a little over 2 kilos (5 lbs) of shredded cabbage will convert the sugar in the cabbage to lactic acid, 'souring' it.

Place a saucer on top of the layers so that it presses down on the cabbage but not on the sides of the casserole dish. Put a weight on the saucer, such as a jam jar containing a few lead sinkers, and let it stand overnight. The next day, discard the brine that will have formed, and rinse the cabbage so that it is not too salty. Pack it loosely in sterilised jars with plastic or glass lids.

Submerge the cabbage in spiced vinegar. My favourite vinegar is cider, yours might be malt. My favourite spices for cabbage are pimento and caraway seed. For maximum preservation, most of the vinegar on the cabbage needs to be unboiled, so boil just a little vinegar with the spice you select and top up the jar with unboiled plain vinegar.

After steeping for a week, the cabbage pickle is ready to eat straight from the jar.

# Pickled Lemons

Old graveyards, abandoned settlements and old stockyard camp sites are often sources of 'escaped' food plants. Anne's recipe, dated 1836, is particularly suitable for the thick-skinned bush lemons found in such neglected places. It also works well for large limes, which turn translucent after the first stage of the process and keep for many months.

*6 lemons*

*cooking salt*

*spiced vinegar (allspice and ginger)*

*30g (2oz) mustard seed*

*2 cloves garlic*

*They should be small, and with thick rinds: rub them with a piece of flannel; then slit them half down in four quarters, but not through to the pulp. Fill the slits with salt hard pressed in, set them upright in a pan for four or five days, until the salt melts; turn them thrice a day in their own liquor, until tender; make enough pickle to cover them, of rape vinegar, the brine of the lemons, Jamaica pepper [allspice], and ginger; boil and skim it; when cold, put it to the lemons, with two ounces of mustard seed, and two cloves of garlic to six lemons. When the lemons are used, the pickle will be useful in fish or other sauces.*

Any vinegar other than balsamic can be used. I use cider vinegar. The liquid, or 'pickle' as Anne calls it, becomes thick like syrup, presumably from pectin soaking out of the pips.

# Pickled Onions

small brown onions

salt

brown malt vinegar spiced with chili, coriander, rosemary, sage, pepper,
   cinnamon, allspice and cloves

bay leaves

white mustard seeds

Select onions of uniform size. Peel off their outer dry skin and trim off the top and the base. Steep the onions overnight in a saturated salt solution (water with as much salt as it will absorb — about 2 cups of salt to 1 cup of water). Boil a small amount of the brown malt vinegar with the spices listed. Bay leaves are traditional as flavouring in pickled onions. They may be boiled with the spices or put in the jars with the mustard seed.

Drain the onions from the brine, drop them into the boiling vinegar and let it return to the boil, then remove it from the fire. Prepare storage jars by placing a few white mustard seeds and some cold unspiced malt vinegar in each. Fill each jar with onions and spiced vinegar and seal.

Pickled onions are ready to eat in two weeks and will store well for months.

# Salade

From my great-great-grandmother Anne's recipe book, dated 1836, comes the following family favourite:

*An excellent and not common pickle called Salade:*

> *onions*
>
> *cucumbers*
>
> *sour apples*
>
> *salt*
>
> *cayenne*
>
> *soy sauce*
>
> *white wine*
>
> *vinegar*

*Fill a pint stone jar with equal quantities of onions, cucumbers, and sour apples all cut into very thin slices, shaking in, as you go on, a tea-spoonful of salt, and three parts of a tea-spoonful of cayenne. Pour in a wineglass of soy, the same of white wine, and fill up the jar with vinegar. It will be fit for use the same day.*

For preserved fish, meats and eggs, see their respective chapters.

# Yeasts & bread — sours

Yeasts are forms of microscopic plant life that reproduce by means of 'buds' from the parent cell. When the cell wall ruptures, spores are released and become airborne natural agents of spontaneous fermentation.

Yeasts have been described as 'truly man's best friend — whoever heard of a dog that could brew beer or make bread?'

Natural or wild yeasts abound in many places, such as potato skins, fresh fruit skins and the skins of dried fruit like raisins, provided they have not been coated in oil. The cosmetic titivation of oiling raisin and sultana skins is done to boost consumer confidence, we are told — apparently we need to be protected from the knowledge that food and life are so closely intermingled.

Wild yeasts can be nurtured in the galley in the form of bread-sour to make bread and cakes, muffins, scones, pikelets and pancakes and so forth, using sourdough bread techniques, as well as ginger beer and sima (a Finnish non-alcoholic ale). On board our trusty old Wharram cat wild yeast for bread making froths and bubbles in one hull, while fresh apple cider vinegar brews in the other. Both are natural ferments easily managed at home. Revive these old skills, and reap the rewards!

Don't be cowed into believing that only commercial yeasts are 'safe' or 'reliable'. Commercial yeast has been selectively developed to work quickly and save time, but the speeding up of the leavening process produces a loaf of lower nutritive value. The slower, sourdough bread-leavening results in the highest nutritive value of the grain being made most readily available for human metabolism.

The further away you sail from a source of fresh eggs and butter the more important your bread-sour becomes. While eggs and butter are to hand, rich cakes, pastry, gnocchi and so on can be made. But dear old faithful bread needs only sour, salt, flour and water.

# A bread-sour called Puck

Years ago I lived in an old house with an overgrown rambling cottage garden that had been planted in the 1930s. It was an Edna Walling garden, with herbs crowding round the kitchen door and gnarled old fruit trees including nectarines and quinces and a plum tree that in summer became a raucous theatre for rainbow lorikeets, whose brilliant plumage merged with the plump, wine-dark purple fruit. The plums were the old variety, bearing a 'bloom' of powdered yeast spores. One evening, I mixed a thin batter of rye bread-flour and water in a bowl, and stood the bowl in the tree overnight. During the night, yeast spores released from the plums were captured by the dew and landed in the batter. There they multiplied and became my rye-sour to leaven my bread. And that is the basis of any bread-sour, whatever the source of the yeast. Once fermentation is established, you simply feed it with flour and water and always hold some back when you use it for bread making or pass some on to a friend to start their own. A bread-sour can live for generations in this way, and travel far.

Years later I shared my rye-sour with Erja Vasumaki and Glenn Horne aboard the 32-foot Ericsson sloop *Aku Ankka*, out of Seattle. Since then Erja has shared it with other cruisers heading to all points of the globe. I wonder how many nautical miles it has covered and how many loaves it has leavened. Our latest mail from *Aku Ankka* arrived from Chagos, in the British Indian Ocean Territory.

A bread-sour becomes a live member of the family, a family pet, and is often bestowed a name. I have known a Celeste and a Hubert. My own precious sour, Puck, lives in a terracotta jar suspended in the galley. The jar must be commodious enough to allow the sour to wax and wane contentedly, as you feed it. Puck's jar has a 2.5 litre (5 pint) capacity.

Warmth, water, flour and sugar make it grow. Cold and salt inhibit its growth. Starved, it will die. North of 18°S it multiplies rapidly and needs frequent feeding. To keep it alive and active feed it half a cup of flour and half a cup of water three times a day.

To make a batch of bread, a portion of the sour culture is removed and added to the other bread-making ingredients, leaving behind enough of the culture so that yeast spores continue to multiply in the terracotta jar.

If the volume of your bread-sour is outgrowing your jar, you can also use it to make cakes, scones, pikelets, pancakes and waffles. In virtually any recipe that asks for milk to combine flour and sugar, any of the following bread-sours can be substituted for the milk.

Confidence in managing a bread-sour grows with practice. Have trust in your bread-sour; it will become your best friend as it tirelessly froths and bubbles, waxes and wanes, smelling yeasty but not 'off'.

## Potato Yeast Sour

'Yest' is the old name for potato yeast in old recipe books, and it must have been commonplace in every family household. To provide your own, simply save the water in which potatoes, yams, kumera (orange-fleshed sweet potato) or taro have been boiled in their skin. When the water cools to blood heat, mix it with enough flour to make a light batter. Let it stand until it froths, then feed it as you would any bread-sour and use it to leaven your bread. The length of time needed for its initial establishment — somewhere between 2 and 4 days — depends on the quality of the flour used and the temperature, preferably somewhere between 20°C and 40°C. Initial establishment takes days, even in the tropics, and is reached when frothing and bubbling begin. Once established it needs only 12 to 24 hours to 'sponge' in a bread recipe.

# Wild Rice Sour

After reading that wild rice had been retrieved from oblivion and rediscovered in a pharaoh's tomb, still viable after thousands of years, I decided to find out what sort of a leavening agent it would make. The ancient Egyptians were famous brewers and bread makers. I saved the unsalted water in which wild rice had been boiled, and, when it cooled to blood heat, added wholemeal flour to the consistency of thin batter. In the tropical warmth this sourdough culture frothed and bubbled with the wildest enthusiasm. Its most astonishing feature is the speed with which it multiplies to leaven bread with a distinctive flavour.

# Rye Sour

Rye and cultured sour cream have an affinity with each other. Rye flour, or the coarser rye meal, combined with sour cream makes excellent bread, once fermentation has been allowed to develop and strengthen over two or three days' initial establishment.

# Chickpea Bread-sour

Save the water in which chickpeas (garbanzos) have been boiled. When it cools to blood heat, add enough wholemeal flour to make a thin batter. Allow it to ferment, and feed it daily for four or five days until it is strong enough to leaven bread, such as a hearth bread like pita.

# Beer Yeast Sour

People like Neville Lloyd on *Songlines*, who home-brew beer aboard cruisers, have on hand a good supply of active yeast for bread leavening — the beer itself, and especially the lees in the bottom of the bottle. Use it, first with a little beer, to form a thick batter with white or wholemeal flour. Let this brew for several hours until it becomes an active ferment.

# Pawpaw Sour

Crushed with a little honey, pawpaw will quickly ferment. Add water and wholemeal flour to make a thin batter, and allow it to continue developing into an agent strong enough to leaven bread. Depending on the temperature, you may need to feed it water and flour twice daily for three days.

# Bread-sour Scones

For this recipe, the bread-sour should be of a thin batter consistency.

>  **2 tablespoons butter**
>
>  **2 cups SR flour**
>
>  **1 teaspoon sugar**
>
>  **pinch of salt**
>
>  **about $^3/_4$ cup bread-sour**

Rub the butter into the flour, sugar and salt, and add enough bread-sour to make a light dough. Bake immediately in a hot oven for 10 minutes.

# Breads

Bread making has been the common realm of ordinary homemakers for countless generations. In traditional practice, Australian Aboriginal women used nardoo grain, a stone quern, water and a campfire to bake hearth bread. There's no high technology or complex equipment needed to bake bread successfully. Ordinary people should not be misled to believe we are incapable of providing healthy food out of our own homes.

Bread is still priced according to its weight; commercial bakers who add whole grain, such as linseed, are adding weight, but not assimilable food value until the grain is crushed. If you want extra roughage, by all means add whole linseed, but a commercial baker's first concern is commerce, and common sense tells you homemade sourdough bread is going to be best. As for cost: the last time I priced the difference, a loaf of commercial rye bread cost $1.60, while a bag of rye meal cost $16.00 and made 100 loaves! Of course, if a well-meaning guest arrives on board clutching a gift that turns out to be a loaf of 'fresh' commercial bread, accept it graciously. It's quite useful as port-hole putty.

Return to the handmade hearth-loaf and regain control over what goes into your bread while you restore significance to the familiar words: 'Give us this day our daily bread.' All the great religions of the world teach reverence for food, from the Christian Bible to the Rig Veda where the hymn to Pitu, the guardian of nourishment, says 'Come hither to us, O Food, auspicious with auspicious help, health-bringing, not unkind, a dear and guileless friend.'

Good quality bread is a meal in itself. As a rule of thumb, the more rustic the recipe the better the bread. Because good quality handmade bread provides such valuable wholefood nourishment, bread may become the largest component in a meal instead of just its decoration or packaging, and you can cut down on the other foods on the plate. Bread and a mug of soup; bread and a little bit of meat or fish; bread and a little bit of greens; bread and jam — and everyone's satisfied. Even simpler is the delicious meal of bread dipped first in olive oil then into a bowl of dukkah.

Anybody interested in good food, anybody who enjoys good food, and certainly anybody concerned about the quality of food, should acquaint themselves with expert literature on the subject of bread, such as *The Natural Tucker Bread Book* by John Downes.

## Sourdough bread making

The logic of bread making is simple. Flour contains protein (gluten) and/or starch, and different flours contain these components in different proportions. For example cornflour, which is ground from maize, contains all starch and no protein. It is the high proportion of gluten in 'hard' flour which, when worked up by kneading the bread dough, provides the strength in the dough structure to trap the bubbles of gas formed as the yeast multiplies and ferments. In order for the bread-sour and flour to grow into an active ferment, it needs to be left to sit quietly in a warm place to 'sponge' for an hour or so. Loosely covered, the yeast feeds on the flour and actively bubbles until it looks like a sponge. The sponge is next mixed with the bulk of the bread ingredients and kneaded well to work up the gluten in the flour. The bread dough is left undisturbed in a warm place to double in size. After 'knocking down' to let the gas escape and forming into loaves, the loaves are again left to sit undisturbed, to 'prove', so that fermentation continues to expand the dough. When the bread is baked the hot oven kills the yeast, but the bubbles remain trapped, and form an important part of the loaf structure.

Different flours also have different water absorbency power, which determines the amount of liquid able to be absorbed by a particular flour. That is why the directions in the recipes that follow are very fluid in terms of measures of flour and liquid. Such quirks of cooking are not life and death situations and there's no need to worry as though it were an apothecary of lethal concoctions. Relax, and have some fun experimenting!

Select your ingredients carefully. I recommend **attar flour** (the finest of wholemeal flour, so fine it feels like silk, available in Asian and Middle Eastern groceries), rye flour and spelt flour for bread making. Unbleached flour is better food value than bleached (which has a longer shelf life). 'Bread making flour' is the term used for flour prepared for commercial bakers. It sounds so appropriate! I strongly suspect that the 'bread-mixes' currently in vogue for domestic electric bread-machines contain additives like 'bread-extender' (a waste product from the cotton-manufacturing industry), and 'mould inhibitor' (a pesticide) for loaf-keeping qualities. You don't need to worry about such products — make a daily batch, and if you really want to keep it, you'll have to keep it hidden.

Recipes for bread abound in ethnic cuisines, ranging from simple **flatbreads** (also called **hearth breads**) like the Greek pita and Lithuanian lavash, to lavish concoctions embracing eggs, fruit and nuts and covered in icing. The practical barefoot rover can bake a batch of rolls with cheese and onion to save adding these later.

Just a little bit of practice with your own yeast, your own oven, and your own crew's preferences will give you the confidence to embellish your own bread recipes.

When is a loaf of bread cooked through?
When a hollow sound is produced if you rap your knuckles on the bottom of the loaf.
A muffled sound is a loaf still gluey in the centre.

# Yeast & Bread

From my mother Lilian Burbury's book, hand-written and dated 1930.

*The yeast:*

*30g (1oz) hops*

*2 medium-sized potatoes*

*3 pints water*

*2 tablespoons sugar*

*1 cup flour*

*Boil hops, potatoes, and water 20 minutes, strain and add sugar. Allow to get quite cold, mix the flour with a little of the liquor, add to the rest of the yeast and bottle. Cork well, using a seasoned bottle.*

*The first trick in making yeast is to get a well-seasoned bottle. It is a good plan to brew yeast in small quantities several times in the same bottle, leaving a little of the old brew in each time. In summer the yeast requires only 8 or 10 hours to ripen, in winter from 20 to 24 hours.*

*The bread:*

*3 kg (6 lbs) flour*

*³/₄ cup of yeast*

*1 cup warm water*

*1 tablespoon salt*

*Put flour in a large basin, make a well in the centre, and pour in the yeast, add the warm water, and mix into a batter. Cover well with flour and stand in a warm place overnight. In* the morning, sprinkle the salt over the flour and add sufficient warm water to the flour to mix all into a light dough. Cover with a cloth to prevent crusting and stand in a warm place again till the dough has risen to twice its original size.

Knead a second time to make the bread of an even texture. Knead till bubbles disappear and dough is elastic to touch, then shape into loaves; again stand until loaves have doubled in size. Put in a very hot oven, decrease heat to moderate and cook 30-40 minutes, until crust is an even brown colour, and a hollow sound is produced when a loaf is rapped on the bottom with the fingers.

# Cream of Tartar Yeast & Bread

Also from Lilian's book.

> *1 tablespoon cream of tartar*
> *1 tablespoon sugar*
> *4 kg (8 lbs) wholemeal flour*
> *1 tablespoon cooking salt*

Mix cream of tartar, sugar and 1 tablespoon flour into a smooth paste with a little warm water and leave overnight. In the morning add 2 cups of warm water, bottle and it will be ready for use at midday. Sufficient for ten tin loaves of bread.

At middFay, to make five loaves, mix 4 kilos of flour with the cooking salt. Make a well in the centre of the flour, add 1 cup of the cream of tartar yeast and 1 cup of warm water. Stir in sufficient flour to make a thick paste, then lightly sprinkle flour on top.

*Stand undisturbed for 6 hours to allow it to 'sponge'.*

*Next, add sufficient warm water to form a good dough, knead it well, taking up the remainder of the flour, and allow to stand overnight in a warm place. Punch it down once, allow to rise again, knead it gently, put into greased tins, and when it is well risen, bake it in a hot oven, reducing the heat to moderate after the first 20 minutes.*

The success of this yeast and bread depends very much on the freshness of the wholemeal used; it's best to use freshly ground flour, used within 6 hours of grinding. The vessel *Largo*, a frequent visitor to the Kimberley, has a crew who gladly grind their own flour to bake their bread.

# Finnish-Style Rye Bread (Finnish Females)

1 cup rye-sour

$1^{1}/_{4}$ cups water (or whey from cottage cheese)

300 ml wholemeal flour

1 tablespoon cooking salt

1 tablespoon molasses

1 tablespoon brown vinegar

300 ml rye flour

Mix the rye-sour with the water (or whey) and wholemeal flour and let this grow into an active ferment; it may need an hour or two to 'sponge', so sit it quietly in a warm place. Cover loosely; when you take a peek it should look like a sponge when ready.

Add cooking salt, molasses and brown vinegar.

Add the rye flour until the dough is of kneading consistency. Tip out of the bowl and knead well, working up the gluten to form an elastic texture. Return the dough to the bowl and allow another 4 to 6 hours rising, or longer in cold weather.

Divide the dough into six portions and knead these separately, taking up more rye off the bench as you go. Shape the loaves into 'Finnish Females' — the size of a bread-and-butter plate with a hole through the center like the axis of a wheel, traditionally decorated in three places with a fork scraped along the radius.

Allow the loaves to 'prove' undisturbed another 10 minutes then bake in a hot oven for about 20 minutes. The relatively thin shape of these loaves and the hole through the centre means they cook evenly and fast.

# Burghul Wheat Bread

300 ml (1$^1$/$_2$ cups) rye-sour

1 cup whey (or water or yoghurt)

1 cup pearled burghul

3 cups wholemeal flour

1 tablespoon salt

Mix the rye sour, whey, pearled burghul and half a cup of the wholemeal flour, and leave to sponge.

Add 2$^1$/$_2$ cups of wholemeal flour and the salt. Knead well, then allow to prove about 6 hours.

Divide into six 'females' as in the previous recipe, and allow a further 10 minutes proving. Bake in a hot oven about 20 minutes.

# Banana Bread

Even when sliced and buttered, three-day old banana bread is practically a cake. By whatever name you choose, it's good tucker.

3 very ripe bananas (black, even!)

1 tablespoon lime juice

$^1/_2$ cup butter

$^1/_2$ cup brown sugar

1$^1/_2$ cups wholemeal flour

$^1/_2$ cup wheatgerm (or oatmeal or semolina)

$^1/_2$ teaspoon salt

$^1/_2$ teaspoon baking soda

$^1/_2$ cup sunflower seeds (or crushed macadamias or chopped dates)

scant teaspoon cream of tartar

Mash the bananas with the lime juice; cream the butter and sugar together; add the bananas and stir in all the dry ingredients to form a stiff batter. Tip it into a greased bread tin and bake for 40 to 45 minutes in a moderate to hot oven. When cooked through, it will start to shrink away from the sides of the tin.

# Brita Bread

The fastest way of whipping up half a dozen scones for unexpected guests. Cruising aboard the Finn sloop *Brita* we always had lots of unexpected visitors. Often the bread supply would run out and I would whip up a few plain scones as a substitute. They taste like damper, and became known as Brita Bread.

>**2 cups SR flour**
>
>**pinch of salt**
>
>**$^3/_4$ cup galley-made yoghurt)**

Add as much galley-made yoghurt to the flour and salt as is needed to form a dough that just leaves the bowl clean. Use a knife to stir in the yoghurt, starting with a little less than you imagine will be enough. Coax the dough into shape, rather than trying to roll it. Bake in the hot Dutch oven as scones, on a tray kept off the bottom. Three pebbles will keep it off the bottom and prevent burning.

# Roti

1 teaspoon celery seed

2 cups fine wholemeal flour (attar flour or a blend of wholemeal and
   a little oatmeal)

salt

$^2/_3$ cup of cold water

30g ghee plus extra ghee for frying

Mix celery seed, flour and a little salt; rub in ghee; add enough water to form a dough. Knead this very well for 10 or 15 minutes, working up the gluten to strengthen the elasticity of the dough. Divide it into eight balls.

Roll each ball out into a disc about the size of a bread-and-butter plate. Cut through the pastry from the centre to the perimeter along the radius and roll each disc into a cone (starting at a cut edge). Fold over the ends of each cone into the centre, making small parcels of dough in which bubbles of air are trapped.

Allow each parcel to rest for at least 10 minutes, then roll out again into a thin disc and shallow fry in hot ghee until lightly browned and cooked through. If all goes well, they should have hollow pockets in them where the bubbles of trapped air expanded in the heat of the cooking.

# Bread-sour Roti

Roti made with an active bread-sour will bubble as they cook because of the yeast in the sour.

> **1 cup bread-sour**
>
> **1 teaspoon salt**
>
> **attar flour (fine wholemeal)**

Put the sour and salt into a bowl and add enough attar flour to knead into an elastic dough. The amount of flour will depend on its water absorbency. Tip the dough onto the bench and knead it for a minute or so, then divide it into sections to roll out into flat rounds roughly the size of a small dinner plate. Cook them immediately by dry-frying them on a hot girdle, turning to brown both sides. Two minutes altogether should see each one done.

# Polenta Bread

Polenta is coarsely ground maize, generally deep yellow in colour.

> **200g (1 cup) polenta**
>
> **4 cups boiling water**
>
> **1 teaspoon salt**

Use a double boiler to avoid having to stir the polenta while it cooks. Put the boiling water, salt and polenta in the top of the double boiler. After 30 minutes the polenta should be a thick porridge.

Spread the porridge out into a greased tin large enough for the depth of the mixture to equal the thickness of a slice of toast. Let it cool and set, then cut it into convenient slices and toast them on a hot cast-iron girdle or grill them.

Alternatively, after the polenta porridge has cooled, flatten small quantities into wafer-thin portions and shallow-fry them crisp.

# Potato Cakes

This basic recipe is easily adapted to different kinds of flour and different kinds of potato, sweet potato or yams.

**cooked potato (or sweet potato or yams)**

**butter**

**salt**

**SR flour**

Precise quantities are impossible to identify, simply because different flours have different water-absorbency powers, and so do different spuds. All the cook needs to do is mash the cooked spud with butter and salt, and then add enough SR flour to form a dry dough. Roll it out lightly to 10 mm thickness, cut it into cocked hat shapes (see page 96) and dry-fry them on a hot girdle or a cast-iron frying pan. Serve them split and buttered hot.

# Sourdough English Muffins

A recipe devised by Erja Vasumaki, aboard *Aku Ankka* out of Seattle, using the rye-sour we shared at Kioloa. Traditional Sunday breakfast aboard *Aku Ankka* is waffles made with the same sour.

> **1 cup sour**
>
> **$1/2$ cup warm water**
>
> **$1/3$ cup milk powder**
>
> **2 cups white flour**
>
> **$1/4$ teaspoon baking soda**
>
> **1 teaspoon salt**
>
> **polenta**

Mix the sour, warm water and milk powder with 1 cup of white flour to a loose dough. Put it to rise to double its size overnight.

In the morning mix together the baking soda, salt and the remainder of the white flour, and add to the above soft dough. Add more flour if necessary to form a pliable dough.

Let it prove to double its size, roll it out to 10 mm thick, cut out circles with an 8 to 10 cm cutter and dust with polenta.

Let rise 20 to 25 minutes, then cook on a heavy frying pan 10 minutes per side. Split with a fork and toast.

# Damper

Damper is the simplest camp-oven bread; its raising agent is baking powder, not yeast. In that respect damper is closer to a scone than hearth bread. Its preparation takes very little time, and it cooks in the Dutch oven or in the coals of a campfire ashore. Traditionally, hard white flour is used. A mixture of white and wholemeal is also successful, but rye flour works best with yeast. This recipe makes one loaf.

> **4 tablespoons butter (or olive oil)**
> **4 cups flour (not rye)**
> **1 tablespoon baking powder**
> **1 teaspoon salt**
> **1½ cups milk (or milk and yoghurt, or sour cream and water)**

Rub the butter or olive oil into the flour, baking powder and salt. Draw it into a dough with the milk, or milk and yoghurt, or sour cream and water. Lactic acid in the soured products helps the rising. The dough does not need to rest or prove. Form it into one loaf and get it into a hot oven for about 30 minutes.

# Biscuits, cakes & other sweet things

Just like bread, homemade biscuits bear scant resemblance to processed varieties. Gingerbread is a classic example: as fast as you bake it, it vanishes! Astonished at the flavour, newcomers to homemade biscuits always ask, 'But what do you put in them?' The answer is simple — real food.

As a last resort if you have no eggs, in recipes for cakes and fancy breads, vinegar can be substituted (a dessertspoonful per egg). Or try the Royal Flying Doctor *Mantle of Safety Cookbook* egg substitute on page 46. Better still, choose a recipe that doesn't need egg!

# Biscuits

## Cheese Straws

To use up leftover cheese and stale bread.

**120g (4oz) grated cheese (hard cheese, or a combination of hard and soft)**

**1 teaspoon mustard powder**

**1 teaspoon salt**

**120g ghee**

**120g plain flour**

**120g breadcrumbs**

**$\frac{1}{2}$ teaspoon dried ground paprika**

**a sharpening of ground black pepper**

Mix the ingredients and draw together into a dough; it should not need any additional liquid, but if it is too dry add a splash of cold water.

Knead it gently and press it out into a shape suitable to be cut into straws about 15 cm long. Spread the straws onto a baking sheet and bake in a moderate oven for about 10 minutes.

Re-cooking leftovers in this way destroys any lurking unwanted bacteria.

# Cheese Rusks

A recipe from my childhood neighbour, Annie Pearson of King Island, widowed at twenty-eight and at eighty-two still dressed in widow's weeds — black hat and veil, black dress and black gloves, handbag, stockings and shoes. Tall, slender, dignified and elegant, as she went gliding by my father would say in hushed reverence: 'There she goes! The ship under full sail!'

> **60g (2oz) butter**
> **250g (8oz) SR flour**
> **60g (2oz) grated hard cheese**
> **1 egg**
> **milk to moisten**
> **pinch of salt and cayenne**

Rub the butter into the flour, salt and cayenne, then add the cheese, egg and milk to make a stiff scone mixture. Handle it lightly. Cut into shapes and bake as scones, then remove from the oven, split open in halves, and return to a slow oven to dry into rusks. Serve buttered with a paste of cheese, mustard and chopped gherkin or pickled cabbage.

# Cocked Hats

Coastal navigation involving bearings taken from three different reference points — an off-shore island, a headland and a lighthouse, for instance — gives three straight lines drawn on the chart, which should all intersect at the navigator's position. An error of even the tiniest proportions, however, will result in the lines not intersecting perfectly, but forming a triangle known to navigators as a 'cocked hat'.

These rusks are cut into triangles before they go into the oven, the cocked hat shape hopefully reminding the cook not to allow them to burn.

>  **2 cups milk**
>  **185g semolina**
>  **60g grated cheese**
>  **30g butter**
>  **salt and pepper**
>  **1 egg yolk**

Put the milk on to boil, stir in the semolina and cook slowly for 10 minutes. This is best done in the double boiler.

Add the cheese and butter, salt and pepper. Take off the fire and add the egg yolk. Turn all onto a plate and, when cold, cut into cocked hat triangles. Sprinkle with a little grated cheese such as parmesan, then bake in a moderate oven until brown. Serve hot.

# Hokey Pokey Biscuits

Nostalgic childhood memories of warm kitchens on cold days include the indulgence of making hokey pokey biscuits, with sticky fingers and lots of mess. How else can children really learn?

> 1 dessertspoon golden syrup or honey
>
> 1 dessertspoon milk
>
> 1 teaspoon baking soda
>
> 120g butter
>
> $^1/_2$ cup sugar
>
> 1 cup flour

Melt the honey or syrup and milk together and let cool. Add the baking soda, stirring until it froths well. Cream the butter and sugar, add the frothy mixture, then the flour. Roll into balls, press with a fork, then bake in a slow oven for about 30 minutes.

# King Island Shortbread

This recipe comes from windswept King Island, in the path of the Roaring Forties; maybe that's why this shortbread is so heavy!

**250g butter**

**2 tablespoons icing sugar**

**2 tablespoons caster sugar**

**2 tablespoons arrowroot (or cornflour)**

**2 cups soft white flour**

With a big bowl, a strong wooden spoon, and a stout wrist, stir together the butter, icing sugar, caster sugar and arrowroot. Add the flour and form into biscuits and bake in a slow oven for about 1 hour.

# Patanela Biscuits

Like the Tasmanian steel schooner *Patanela*, listed as missing, these simply disappear without trace, yet we feel sure someone knows more than they care to tell.

**200g butter**

**120g caster sugar**

**250g plain flour**

**2 teaspoons ground ginger**

**pinch of salt**

**25g chopped candied peel**

**1 teaspoon ground coriander seed (optional)**

Cream together the butter and sugar until it is pale and fluffy. Fold in the flour, ginger and salt then add the candied peel, and a teaspoon of ground coriander seed if you want extra flavour.

Knead these ingredients lightly into a smooth dough ('soft' biscuit flour will not contain much gluten, therefore your biscuit dough will not have the elasticity of bread dough).

Using your hands, roll the dough out into a long sausage about 25 mm thick. Cut it into lengths about 50 mm long, and transfer them onto a greased baking sheet. Now squash each one a little, using three fingers to flatten the dough gently into a biscuit shape. Bake them in a moderate oven for about 20 minutes.

# Plain 'Table Water' Biscuits

Savoury biscuits do not need to be symmetrically shaped or extravagantly packaged to taste good and be good for you. Bread-sour will provide delicious crisp biscuits, dry-fried on the girdle at medium heat until they are cooked to a crisp.

> **1 cup sour**
>
> **teaspoon salt**
>
> **flour (any sort or combination)**

Add enough flour to the sour and salt to work it into an elastic dough. There's no need to wait for the dough to rise; just pinch off sections to roll out wafer thin and dry-fry to a crisp. If they balloon up too much, puncture them as they cook.

The sour flavour and nutritive satisfaction beats commercial biscuits every time, not to mention the satisfaction of the reward of doing it yourself. Rye flour is especially good for savoury biscuits.

# Sea Biscuits

My brother Alan Scott, baker and wood-fired brick bread-oven builder in California, concocted this recipe, which is included in the *Laurel's Kitchen Bread Book* of the Blue Mountains Centre of Meditation.

> $^1/_2$ **cup wheat grain suitable for sprouting**
>
> **1 tablespoon oil**
>
> $^1/_2$ **teaspoon salt**
>
> $^1/_2$ **teaspoon baking soda**
>
> **1 teaspoon caraway seeds**
>
> **1 cup rye flour**

In the tropics, sprout the wheat for two days only (use the sprouts before green shoots appear). Grind the sprouts through a hand-mincer. Mix in the oil, salt, soda, caraway seeds and enough rye flour to make a stiff paste. Break off golf-ball sized pieces and roll each one out wafer thin.

Bake on a dry heavy frying pan, or the girdle, allowing about 5 minutes each side. Alternatively, bake them in a very slow oven until lightly browned.

# Semolina Biscuits

500g sugar

500g butter

250g semolina

4 tablespoons ground almonds

3 teaspoons rosewater

50g plain flour

Cream together the butter and sugar; gradually beat in all the semolina, the almond meal and the rose water. Fold in the flour. Place dessertspoonful-size dollops of the mixture onto a greased tray, leaving room for the mixture to expand as it heats. Bake in a moderate oven for about 20 minutes.

# Wafers

To use as edible spoons with fruit salad or rum sillabub. This quantity makes enough for a feast (about sixty) but since crisp biscuits rapidly grow limp in humid weather, it is more prudent to halve the recipe than try to store them.

> 1 teaspoon baking soda
>
> 1 tablespoon cold water
>
> $^1/_2$ cup citrus juice
>
> 2 cups flour
>
> 1 teaspoon zest of any citrus fruit
>
> $^1/_2$ cup butter
>
> 1 cup caster sugar

Dissolve the baking soda in the water, add the citrus juice, then add alternately with flour and rind-zest to creamed butter and sugar. Spread mixture wafer thin onto a well-greased baking sheet, and bake quickly (maybe 5 to 10 minutes) in a moderate oven. I use a leather-worker's tool, like a miniature spiked pizza cutting-wheel, to mark the wafers into sections ready to break apart easily when crisp.

*Cakes & Tarts*

# Auntie Min's Cake

Auntie Min, born in 1872, lived at Inglewood in Tasmania, where a batch of bread for the station homestead, baked once a week in the wood-fired bread oven, was fifty loaves— and Tassie loaves are twice the size of mainland loaves! Cakes went into the oven after the bread came out, then fruit was stewed, baked custards set, and finally the kindling for the next week's fire was set to dry.

> 185g (6oz) butter
>
> 1 cup white sugar
>
> 1 egg
>
> $^1/_2$ teaspoon almond essence
>
> 1 teaspoon vanilla essence
>
> 2 teaspoons brown malt vinegar
>
> 1 cup milk
>
> 1 teaspoon baking soda
>
> 250g (8oz) dried fruit (usually sultanas)
>
> 2 cups plain flour

Beat the butter and sugar to a cream. Add the unbeaten egg, almond essence, vanilla essence and vinegar. Next add the milk in which the baking soda has been dissolved, then the dried fruit and the plain flour. Bake in a moderate oven for 40 minutes.

# Basic Fruitcake by volume

Homemade fruitcake is a boon on a cruise. Every small piece is a concentrated source of energy and delight, especially on the dogwatch. The keeping quality of fruitcake is legendary. In past generations, the top tier of the wedding cake was saved for the first christening twelve months later. To help preserve fruitcake in the tropics, paint the outside with brandy, and paint the cut surface, likewise, every time you cut some away.

> 1 cup butter
>
> 1 cup sugar
>
> 3 eggs
>
> $\frac{1}{2}$ cup milk
>
> 1 teaspoon baking soda
>
> 2 teaspoons cream of tartar
>
> 3 cups plain flour
>
> 2 cups dried fruit
>
> $\frac{1}{2}$ cup almonds

Cream the butter and sugar; beat the eggs and add to them the milk in which has been dissolved the baking soda and cream of tartar. Combine with the butter and sugar, add the flour, and last of all the fruit and nuts. Bake in a moderate oven for 90 minutes.

*To make it easier to distribute the fruit evenly throughout the cake mixture when making a fruitcake, first coat the fruit in some of the measured flour.*

# Potter's Fruitcake

Angela Bakker, whose ancestors include the infant born aboard the *Skelton* in 1820, concentrates on her first love, pottery, and makes good use of short cuts like this recipe when it comes to cooking.

> 1 cup SR flour
>
> 395 ml tin condensed milk
>
> 375g mixed dried fruit and nuts

Stir all ingredients together and bake in a loaf tin in a moderate oven for about 2 hours.

*Brandy Sauce (page 218) will turn fruitcake into a lavish dessert.*

# Eggless Legless Cake

Quite an acceptable cake, despite the fact that it contains no egg.

> 60g (4oz) butter
>
> 2 cups SR flour
>
> 2 cups dark brown sugar
>
> 1 cup milk
>
> 1 teaspoon baking soda
>
> handful of walnuts
>
> fresh grated nutmeg

Rub the butter into the flour, then add the sugar. Divide this mixture in half and pack one half down into the bottom of the cake tin, pressing it down to form the base like a biscuit-based crust.

To the other half, add the milk in which the baking soda has been dissolved. Don't panic when this seems to become too sloppy! Pour it carefully onto the first half in the tin, sprinkle walnuts on top, and a generous grating of fresh nutmeg. Bake the cake in a moderate oven for about 40 minutes, until the surface is firm. The crust will have risen up the sides.

# Her Majesty's Date Cake

Dark and moist cake which keeps fresh.

**1 cup chopped dates**

**1 teaspoon baking soda**

**1 cup sugar**

**120g butter**

**1 egg**

**1$^1/_2$ cups plain flour**

**$^1/_2$ teaspoon of salt**

**1 teaspoon vanilla**

**1 teaspoon baking powder**

**$^1/_2$ cup sunflower seeds or walnuts**

**a pinch each of cinnamon, nutmeg and mace**

Pour a cup of boiling water over the dates mixed with baking soda. Let it rest for 20 minutes.

Combine the rest of ingredients to make a cake batter. Stir in the dates, and don't worry if it seems too sloppy a mixture. Bake in a moderate oven for about 40 minutes. When it's done, it will be starting to shrink away from the sides of the cake tin.

# Oatcakes

Best cooked in patty-pan cases, or else aluminium drink cans cut in half.

**1 cup rolled oats**

**³/₄ cup thin bread-sour (or milk and vinegar)**

**¹/₂ cup wholemeal flour**

**1 teaspoon baking powder**

**¹/₂ teaspoon salt**

**1 tablespoon brown sugar**

**1 egg yolk (or a whole egg)**

Soak the rolled oats in the bread-sour for 1 hour. (Milk soured by the addition of one dessertspoon of cider vinegar can be used instead of bread-sour.)

Mix together the wholemeal flour, baking powder, salt and brown sugar. Add the yolk, or whole egg, to the oats; combine this with the dry ingredients to make a thick batter. Half-fill your greased containers and bake in a fairly hot oven for about 20 minutes. Makes a baker's dozen.

# Ocean Passage Cake

This cake needs neither milk nor eggs.

        **120g raisins**

        **60g dates**

        **60g currants**

        **30g preserved ginger**

        **120g butter**

        **120g brown sugar**

        **$\frac{1}{2}$ cup water**

        **1 teaspoon mixed mace, nutmeg and allspice**

        **250g SR flour**

        **pinch of salt**

        **1 teaspoon baking soda**

Put the fruit, butter, sugar, water and spice into a pan. Bring to the boil and let simmer for 10 minutes. Set aside to cool. Measure the flour and salt into a basin, stir in the fruit, and lastly the baking soda dissolved in a dessertspoon of water. Scrape it all into a greased bread tin and bake in a moderate oven for about 1 hour.

# Tea Cake

1 egg

1/2 cup sugar

1/2 teaspoon vanilla

1/2 cup milk

1 tablespoon melted butter

1 cup SR flour

cinnamon and brown sugar mix

Separate the white from the yolk of the egg and beat the white stiffly. Add the sugar and continue beating. Add the vanilla, egg yolk, milk and melted butter, and fold in the flour. Pour this batter into a shallow greased tin and bake in a moderate oven for 20 to 25 minutes. Before it cools, brush with more melted butter and sprinkle liberally with the cinnamon and brown sugar mix.

# Curd Tart

The contemporary name for this kind of tart is 'cheesecake' and recipes currently in vogue call for processed cream cheese. Make your own curds instead, and relish the rewards. Homemade cheese using the rennet from the lining of a chicken giblet is very superior indeed.

sweet shortcrust pastry

200g fresh curds

100g caster sugar

50g currants

2 eggs

nutmeg

Line a tart plate or flan dish with sweet shortcrust pastry.

Mix together the fresh curds, caster sugar and currants and slip in the 2 eggs without too much beating. Pour this into the tart plate and grate fresh nutmeg over the surface. Bake in a moderate to hot oven for about 20 minutes, until the filling is firm.

# Sweet Shortcrust Pastry

Rich sweet pastry homemade from butter, egg yolk, unbleached white flour, lemon juice and sugar is another of those old-fashioned concoctions which take only minutes to prepare, yet leave indelible, lifelong memories of what food should be. This piecrust promises aromatic, flavourful, melt-in-the-mouth satisfying nourishment.

120g butter

185g plain flour

pinch of salt

2 tablespoons icing sugar

teaspoon lemon juice (or pinch of cream of tartar)

1 egg yolk

$^1/_4$ cup cold water (more or less)

Cut or rub the butter lightly into the flour and salt; add the sugar and lemon juice, stirring with a knife. Use the knife to make a 'well', drop in the yolk and start drawing in the flour, adding cold water and working quickly to draw it all together into a paste, leaving the sides of the bowl clean. Don't knead it, keep it light.

For tarts, without a fridge you can't let sweet pastry 'rest' as experts recommend. In the tropics just press your fresh pastry straight into the pie dish and **bake blind** in a hot oven (cover with greaseproof paper and weigh down with dried beans so the pastry will not balloon up), then add jam and nuts, or stewed fruit, or treacle, or uncooked fruit like bananas topped with brown sugar and mace, and return it to a moderate oven. Twenty minutes should see it done, depending on how thick you have made the crust.

# Treacle Tart

**250g wholemeal flour**

**1 teaspoon baking powder**

**pinch salt**

**60g butter**

**3 tablespoons treacle or golden syrup**

**pinch of citric acid**

**$^2/_3$ cup soft white breadcrumbs**

**cinnamon and nutmeg**

**1 dessertspoon sesame seeds**

Mix the flour, baking powder, salt and butter with enough cold water (about $^1/_4$ cup) to draw it together into a light dough. Roll out the pastry and line a pie plate.

Prepare a filling with the treacle (golden syrup is second best) warmed and blended with

1 dessertspoon of water to which has been added a pinch of citric acid and the soft white breadcrumbs. Add spices, such as cinnamon and nutmeg, and the sesame seed. Pour the filling into the pastry case and bake in a moderate oven for about 25 minutes.

# Fruit Tart Crumble Mixture

To pack atop fruit tarts and extend them to feed twice as many people.

> **1 cup SR flour**
> **$^1/_2$ cup brown sugar**
> **$^1/_4$ cup butter**
> **spice (e.g. coriander seed with apple; cardamom with mango)**

Mix the flour and brown sugar, and cut in the butter. Add spice and pack the mixture over the tart and bake in a moderate to hot oven. It should rise and go crunchy.

*Puddings & other sweet things*

# Foxtrot Chocolate Pudding

In the phonetic alphabet FOXTROT is a coded marine message saying 'communicate with me'. When relationships get strained within the confines of a small cruising boat, the delicious flavour of chocolate might be the answer.

$^1/_4$ **cup butter**

$^1/_2$ **cup sugar**

**1 egg**

$^1/_2$ **cup milk**

**1 tablespoon cocoa powder**

**1 cup SR flour**

$^1/_2$ **cup sugar**

**1 tablespoon cocoa powder**

Melt the butter, add the sugar, beaten egg, milk, sifted cocoa and flour. Spread the mixture into a greased casserole dish.

Sprinkle sugar and cocoa for sauce over the surface and, with care, pour $1^1/_2$ cups of boiling water over all. Bake in a moderate oven for 30 to 40 minutes.

# Sawdust Pudding

    3—4 cups stewed apples

    50g butter

    cinnamon

    sugar (optional)

    60g butter

    2 cups dry breadcrumbs

Stew some apples in a very little water, add a lump of butter and a little cinnamon, and sugar if needed for flavour.

Melt butter, stir in breadcrumbs and brown them a little. Spread a layer of the crumbs in the bottom of a casserole dish. Fill the dish with alternate layers of stewed apple and crumbs, finishing with a top layer of crumbs. Bake in a moderate oven for about 20 minutes.

# Snug Cove Pudding

    Batter:

        1 cup flour

        $^1/_2$ teaspoon baking soda

        1 teaspoon cream of tartar

        pinch of salt

        $^1/_2$ cup sugar

        1 cup raisins

$^1/_2$ cup milk

spice such as mace, cinnamon, cloves, nutmeg

Sauce:

2 tablespoons treacle (or honey)

2 cups boiling water

1 tablespoon butter

Combine the batter ingredients and tip into a greased pie dish.

Combine the treacle, boiling water and butter into a sauce and pour it carefully over the batter. Bake in a moderate oven for about 30 minutes. Best eaten hot.

# Caramel Fingers

A favourite recipe of my grandmother, Elsie Burbury, born 1875, a person beloved, respected, lamented. Tasmanians still speak of her cakes and pastry as legendary.

120g (4oz) butter

120g (4oz) white sugar

vanilla

1 egg

1 cup SR flour

$^3/_4$ cup chopped dates

$^3/_4$ cup chopped walnuts

Heat the butter and sugar together and stir until well dissolved and caramelised. Take off the fire and add vanilla, egg, flour, dates and nuts, stirring it all together to make a thick batter. Spread this into a shallow tin and bake in a moderate oven for about 20 minutes. Cut into 'fingers' when cooled.

# Pikelets

Pikelets take very little time to prepare and need no eggs or milk. Eat them before they get cold, spread with a little honey or jam.

**1 cup plain flour**

**1 tablespoon milk powder**

**1 tablespoon honey**

**pinch of salt**

**1 teaspoon baking soda**

**$^1/_2$ teaspoon cream of tartar in 2 tablespoons boiling water**

Place flour, milk powder, honey and salt in a bowl and mix with enough water to make a thick batter. Blend baking soda and cream of tartar with boiling water and add to the batter. The mixture should be a smooth medium-thick consistency, so add more water if necessary.

Grease the girdle and get it well warmed. Drop tablespoonfuls of batter onto the girdle and let them bubble and set before turning each one to brown both sides.

# Sandesh

A traditional Indian steamed cottage cheese dessert adapted for shipboard stores. This recipe uses galley-made sweetened condensed milk in place of egg.

**Sweetened condensed milk:**

$^3/_4$ **cup white sugar**

**1 cup full cream milk powder**

**Curds:**

**4$^1/_2$ cups milk**

**1 teaspoon citric acid**

**2 tablespoons bread-sour or galley-made yoghurt**

**cardamom seeds**

**slivered almonds**

Bake blind a flan case, using sweet shortcrust pastry.

For the filling, first prepare some sweetened condensed milk by dissolving the sugar in half a cup of boiling water; when it cools, add the milk powder.

To make the cheese curds, scald the milk and curdle it by adding a scant teaspoon of citric acid once it has cooled to about blood heat. Stir thoroughly, then strain it through a colander lined with a linen tea towel. Save the whey (the 'water') for scones or bread; let the curds drain really well, for maybe 30 minutes.

Take the curds, the sweetened condensed milk (just under half a cup), the bread-sour or yoghurt and a few cardamom seeds for extra flavour. Blend this together and spread it into the flan case; sprinkle some slivered almonds on top.

Cook it by steaming it, standing on a rack inside the Dutch oven, which has been quarter filled with water. Twenty minutes steaming should be enough to set it, ready to eat hot or cold.

# Traditional Scones

1 tablespoon butter

2 cups SR flour

pinch of salt

teaspoon sugar

$^3/_4$ cup milk (or cream, sour cream, whey, bread-sour, water or flat beer)

Rub the butter into the flour. Add salt and sugar and enough milk to form a soft dough. Spread the dough out onto the bench to a thickness of about 20 mm, suitable to be cut into scone sizes, and bake in a hot oven for about 20 minutes.

# Singin' Hinnies

Also called Cumberland girdle cakes — a hot girdle makes them 'sing'.

375g SR flour

pinch of salt

180g butter

1 cup currants

about $^1/_2$ cup reconstituted milk powder, double strength

Mix the flour and salt, then rub in the butter until free from lumps. Add the currants and mix to a soft dough with the powdered milk.

Press the dough lightly onto a cutting board, spreading it out to a thickness of about 10 mm. Cut it into scone-sized sections and cook them for about 8 minutes each side on a hot, greased girdle.

# Dalken Dough Pie Pastry

To make a lid for stewed fruit pies.

**250g flour**

**180g butter (unsalted is best)**

**60g caster sugar**

**pinch salt**

**3 tablespoons sour cream**

Rub the butter into the flour, add the sugar and salt, draw it together with the sour cream and add a very little water if necessary. No raising agent is needed because the lactic acid in the sour cream makes it light enough. If your stores don't extend as far as the luxury of sour cream, substitute bread-sour and keep your bread-sour cycling.

# Wishful Custard

Genuine custard must have egg yolk, but when eggs are scarce a substitute custard sauce can be made from milk, sugar and arrowroot.

**1 heaped tablespoon arrowroot**

**2 cups milk**

**1$^1/_2$ tablespoons sugar**

**1 teaspoon vanilla flavouring**

**tiny pinch salt**

Put the arrowroot in a basin and use some of the milk to blend it into a thin cream. Heat the remainder of the milk with the sugar, stirring until it reaches simmering point. Pour the hot milk onto the arrowroot and stir to blend it well. It will thicken into a custard sauce but does not need to boil. As it cools, add vanilla flavouring and salt.

See also Pavlova and Rum Sillabub.

# Beans

There are a great number of books relating to vegetarian diets and anyone seriously interested in the complexities of beans and grains and complementary proteins can find instruction and enlightenment in excellent publications devoted entirely to these specialities.

Dried beans and whole grains store well aboard a cruising yacht and provide such excellent food value they deserve our reverent respect. Moreover, it may astonish you to see the saving in weight and volume between dried beans and tins of three bean mix or baked beans.

Recent additions to supermarket shelves are precooked beans and lentils, vacuum packed in strong plastic. These are excellent value as shipboard stores because they require neither refrigeration nor cooking. Their packaging is lighter than tin, and does not rust. However, they are still heavier than dried beans.

It is in the preparation of beans that a pressure cooker really excels. Cooking beans without a pressure cooker involves pre-soaking the dried beans overnight. In the tropics, and without refrigeration, this length of time is enough to start fermentation — something the cook does not want. With a pressure cooker, not only is cooking time so dramatically reduced, more importantly to the barefoot rover, fuel is saved.

With or without a pressure cooker, beans need three or four times their volume of water in which to cook. The table below shows the dramatic difference in time (and therefore fuel) taken to cook.

|                              | Boiling | Pressure Cooker |
| ---------------------------- | ------- | --------------- |
| lentils, split peas          | 1 hour  | 10—15 minutes   |
| navy, kidney, soy, black beans | 2 hours | 20—25 minutes |
| adzuki, mung beans           | 3 hours | 30—35 minutes   |
| chickpeas (garbanzos)        | 4 hours | 45 minutes      |

These times are for a pressure cooker that will produce high pressure (10 lbs on my old model). For cookers that produce less pressure, add 10 minutes to the cooking time. To use a pressure cooker, measure the water needed, bring it to the boil, add the rinsed beans, seal the cooker, bring it to pressure and then start measuring the time.

Ken and Barbara Beashel of *Australia Two* America's Cup fame, and of the cruising ketch *Mother Goose*, first convinced me of the virtues of pressure cookers. I had not realised just how versatile they are, and what a boon on a cruiser. Barb showed me how to reduce the total cooking time of wild ducks by first giving them a burst under pressure, then adding flavouring such as juniper berries, mace and cinnamon, and then braising. And is it port or starboard, starboard or port, that's so distinctive on *Gretel*? I know it's one or the other.

# Baked Beans

Baked beans are best known to Australians as tinned by Heinz. They are navy beans cooked in tomato sauce. How easy to open a tin, but how much easier on a cruise to buy, carry and stow only dried beans and tomato paste to make your own!

> **1 cup dried navy beans**
>
> **chopped fried onions**
>
> **tomato paste**
>
> **Italian herbs**

Cook the navy beans in the pressure cooker for 20 to 25 minutes, then transfer them into a casserole dish and smother them with the onion, tomato paste and herbs. Or the sauce could be leftovers from a baked dinner — meat, veges, gravy. Bake long and slow to mushy perfection.

# Deep South Baked Beans

> **1 cup dried navy beans**
>
> **ham bone (or smoked hock)**
>
> **1 tablespoon molasses**
>
> **black pepper**

The ultimate in traditional beans, from the deep south of the United States, involves boiling the beans with a ham bone, then baking them with molasses and black pepper. Navy beans are indisputably a first-class meal extender with a huge margin of error where time is concerned. Baked beans have the patience of Job, as they quietly plump in the oven.

# Bluewater Lasagne

Adapt the well-loved lasagne to suit a tropical galley, substituting cooked beans (such as soy) for meat, and sweet potato or pawpaw for tomato.

> **lasagne ribbons**
>
> **cooked soy beans**
>
> **white sauce**
>
> **mashed sweet potato (kumera)**
>
> **pawpaw**
>
> **beef stock cube**
>
> **tomato paste**
>
> **Italian herbs (basil, thyme, oregano, sage, pine nuts)**
>
> **grated parmesan (or any hard cheese)**

Build up a casserole of layers of pre-cooked lasagne pasta; cooked beans (with or without a beef stock cube); white sauce; pasta ribbons again; mashed kumera and pawpaw mixed with tomato paste and herbs. Repeat the layers, ending with a top layer of white sauce. Sprinkle with grated parmesan. Add a little extra water to plump the pasta, and bake the dish slowly for 30 minutes.

# Falafel

Falafel are bean patties, a Middle Eastern dish. Prepare the mixture early, and give it enough time to develop its full flavour before re-frying and serving.

> 1 cup mashed potato or sweet potato, or cooked yellow split peas (moong dhal)
>
> 3 cups cooked and minced chickpeas (garbanzos)
>
> 1 cup chopped and lightly fried onion
>
> fresh or dried herbs such as parsley and coriander leaves
>
> 3 tablespoons peanut oil
>
> $1/4$ cup sesame seed or wheatgerm
>
> 1 tablespoon yoghurt
>
> 1 clove crushed garlic
>
> 1 tablespoon salt
>
> cayenne pepper
>
> tamarind or lime juice

Combine the ingredients, using sufficient of the tamarind juice or lime juice to bind them together if the mixture is too dry. Form into patties and shallow-fry quickly in ghee or peanut oil. Egyptian tradition serves these with fresh greens and a garlic sauce like taratoor.

# Lima Bean Tuna Curry

1 cup diced fresh bluefin tuna

1 cup chopped liver and roe (or milt) from the fish

1 dessertspoon curry powder

1 tablespoon Squid Brand fish sauce

1 cup coconut cream

1$^{1}/_{2}$ cups cooked lima beans

1 green apple (or pickled limes or bush lemons)

Fry together, gently, the tuna meat and chopped liver and roe. Stir in the curry powder and fish sauce. Allow it to boil, then stir in the coconut cream and cooked lima beans. Serve with sliced raw green apple.

# Shipboard Chickpeas

Simple rustic concoctions like this recipe for chickpeas illustrate the huge saving in weight of stores on board a cruiser. Here a cup of chickpeas weighing roughly 175g will easily feed two people with a healthy appetite. How far would one tin of baked beans go, weighing 454g?

> **1 cup dried chickpeas**
>
> **salt**
>
> **crushed fresh garlic**
>
> **fresh grated ginger**
>
> **olive oil**
>
> **hearth bread**
>
> **kang kong**

Cook the dried chickpeas in the pressure cooker for 45 minutes. Save the water in which they were cooked. Mince or mash the peas and add salt, garlic and a whisper of ginger. Stir in some olive oil to make a creamy texture. Toast some hearth bread, such as Finnish Females made with burghul, tear the toast into bite-sized pieces and arrange them in soup bowls. Sprinkle the reserved bean stock liberally over the bread. Now dollop on the chickpea puree and sprinkle with chopped kang kong to add green value.

# Grains

Grains are familiar as rice, wheat, corn and oats, though not so familiar as **burghul** (crushed wheat kernels), buckwheat and millet.

Grains subdivide into two groups: whole grains and partly processed grains, the latter including rolled oats, hulled millet, pearled barley, pearled burghul, and cracked wheat.

In a galley with no refrigeration, whole grains store even better than cracked or milled grain. That's why I take whole wheat aboard and crack only what's needed when I make tabouli. My hand-operated cast-iron mincer (looking like it's left over from the Boer War) cracks grain, minces sprouted wheat for sea biscuits, minces fish and onion for kibbeh, and silently tends to a score of other food-processor tasks.

# Thermos cooking

Grains, especially pearled burghul, pearled barley and rolled oats, can be 'cooked' in a wide-necked thermos by merely measuring the volume of grain, adding the appropriate volume of boiling water (or fish stock, or boiling milk), and leaving the thermos closed. Oats and burghul need only 20 minutes; pearled barley a little longer. This is an extremely economical method of barefoot cooking, especially in a small galley where there may only be one burner.

The grains can be a combination of various whole grains, even grains needing different lengths of cooking time. Overnight the thermos patiently and adequately cooks and keeps warm a blend of millet, buckwheat, brown rice or whatever you fancy. You may gasp, but brown rice and wild rice cook adequately in a thermos.

# Dry-roasting

A variation in the preparation of some grains is to **dry-roast** them (in a nonstick pan, without oil or with a mere whiff of oil) before boiling. Burghul and buckwheat both gain an extra depth of flavour this way. For authentic Italian risotto, arborio rice is fried in a sprinkle of olive oil until it 'shrieks', after which the liquid is added and the grain boiled.

# Rule-of-thumb grain cooking

When it comes to pressure cooking, grains are different from beans. Pressure cooking is not generally recommended for grains in case the vent of the cooker becomes clogged.

If you can't wait for the thermos method, use a double boiler or improvise one with a basin and a saucepan. The basin must have a lid.

There is no need to include salt as the grain cooks. Salt can be added last as you assemble the ingredients of a dish.

Get some water boiling in the bottom of the boiler, put the grain in the top part of the boiler and add boiling water (for volume, see the table below) onto the grain. Close the lid and don't bother stirring, it won't stick to the pot. Just watch that the bottom section doesn't boil dry.

An approximate volume and time guide for cooking grains:

| One cup uncooked grain | Water | Time |
| --- | --- | --- |
| buckwheat | 2 cups | 20 minutes |
| burghul | 2 cups | 20 minutes |
| rolled oats | 2 cups | 20 minutes |
| polenta | 4 cups | 30 minutes |
| millet | 3 cups | 45 minutes |
| brown rice | 2 cups | 1 hour |
| wild rice | 3 cups | 1 hour |
| pearled barley | 3 cups | 90 minutes |

Since variety is the spice of life, a good selection of grains makes a more interesting galley. For the barefoot rover, all grains have several things in common: they store long term without refrigeration, they take up little space, they weigh little and feed many. In desperate circumstances they may be eaten raw, unlike beans which must be boiled to eliminate indigestible toxins.

A fried rice dish offers the chance to combine a great variety of flavours and tidbits, leftovers and favourites; so, too, a dish of mixed grains offers the chance to be just as versatile, or to extend to luxuries such as pine nuts.

Certain characteristics of different grains become apparent as they become more familiar.

For instance, buckwheat seems to go with fava beans (dried broad beans) and bacon, while rolled oats cooked with milk still goes with brown sugar and cinnamon.

Rice surely needs no introduction, even if your total experience of it is no more than 'lovely rice pudding for dinner again!' in A. A. Milne's poem. Versatile and predictable, rice is readily available in different varieties for different purposes: long-grain for Asian stir-fry, sticky rice for desserts and confectionery, sushi rice for sushi rolls, arborio rice for risotto, wild rice with its distinct flavour and texture.

E. Buchman Ewald's much loved and dog-eared classic, *Recipes for a Small Planet*, makes note of the advice that one cup of rice needs two cups of water in which to cook, yet two cups of rice need only three and a half cups of water. Rice is a special grain which really does benefit from some Asian culinary finesse.

# Small Planet Pressure-cooked Rice

*Recipes for a Small Planet* describes a method of cooking rice which really appeals to me.

*Frankie's method to avoid sticking and other tricks: Put 2 to 3 inches of water into the pressure cooker and start it heating. Put the grains in a small stainless steel bowl (or even in a tin can or two) that will fit easily into the cooker without obstructing any vents. Fill the bowl with water to an inch above the grain. Put the bowl in the cooker, cover and bring to fifteen pounds of pressure.*

[Measure the length of cooking time from when the valve starts to rotate.]

*When it's done you will have a bowl of rice! The trick when using this method is to put beans in the 2 to 3 inches of water that are on the bottom of the cooker. Your beans and grains are both cooked!*

Time needed for pressure cooking one cup of rice is 20 minutes.

# Tabouli

The most authentic tabouli uses freshly cracked wheat, but pearled burghul may also be used. It is also best with fresh tomato and plenty of fresh mint and parsley, but those ingredients are often not readily available on a cruising boat. A fair substitute can be offered in the following recipe.

> 3 cups whey or water
>
> 1 teaspoon salt
>
> white pepper to taste
>
> 1½ cups raw cracked wheat
>
> 2 tomatoes (preferably Roma), roughly chopped
>
> 3 tablespoons virgin olive oil
>
> 3 tablespoons lemon juice or tamarind juice
>
> 1 clove garlic, crushed
>
> 1 large white onion, finely chopped
>
> 1 teaspoon dried mint flakes
>
> 1 cup chopped kang kong
>
> the seeds from one green cardamom pod (they should be black and sticky)

Bring the whey to the boil with the salt and pepper, add the grain and wait until it returns to the boil. Take it off the fire, close the lid of the pot and let it stand undisturbed for about 15 minutes or longer if you don't like your grain 'al dente'. Drain off any remaining liquid and immediately stir in the dried mint. When the grain has cooled stir in the remaining ingredients and add more salt if necessary.

# Bluefin and Burghul

Trolling a lure astern of a moving sailing boat easily catches bluefin tuna. A very average catch could weigh 6 kilos.

> bluefin tuna
>
> chopped onion
>
> peanut oil
>
> 1 heaped teaspoon seasoning mix (salt, chicken extract, black pepper,
> garlic, sugar, onion, rosemary, paprika, turmeric, capsicum, citric acid,
> coriander seed, ginger and celery seed)
>
> 2 cups fish-head stock or plain water
>
> 1 cup raw burghul grain

Save the heart, liver and stomach pouch from your catch. Empty the stomach pouch, turn it inside out and clean it well. Slice these three pieces of offal and fry them gently with a chopped onion in some peanut oil. Use a pan that has a tightly fitting lid. Any small trimmings from filleting the fish may be added also.

Stir in seasoning mix (you could substitute a shop-bought mix such as Master Foods Moroccan Seasoning).

Pour in fish-head stock or plain water. When the stock comes to the boil, add the burghul and stir until the mixture returns to the boil. Take it off the fire and close the lid tightly. Leave it to swell the grain for about 20 minutes.

Serve with a few fresh leaves of sweet potato or kang kong, and sourdough flatbread cooked on the girdle while you wait for the grain to plump.

# Greens + other fresh produce

Pirates, buccaneers, privateers, corsairs — whether, in your own imagination, you embellish them with romanticism or fanatical freedom, or condemn them as worthless social outcasts, one thing is sure: shipboard life in their day, and in the days of great seafarers like Magellan, was blighted by scurvy, the bane of lengthy voyaging.

There is a better understanding today about the importance of balance and the essential value of vitamins contained in fresh fruit and vegetables. A diet of salt pork, hard tack and rum is clearly inadequate. The question remains, however: how can the fresh essentials be consistently included in a tropical galley without refrigeration? There are three basic solutions: grow them on board, carry veges that store well, and gather wild greens.

# Live greens

Bean sprouts such as mung beans and alfalfa are not easily managed in the high humidity of the tropics. The climate fosters unwanted fermentation and the sprouts quickly turn to mush. The Top End substitute is to grow live greens such as sweet potato (*Ipomoea batatas*) and kang kong (*I. aquatica*). One large sweet potato standing in a container of water will sprout from several different places and produce long vines. Browse the leaves just behind the growing tips.

**Kang kong**, recently awarded the more fashionable name Japanese water spinach, is a fast growing, rambling vine with edible white flowers and green leaves the colour of English spinach but longer and more slender. Like sweet potato, it grows in water without soil. Freshly browsed leaves have a spicy flavour which is often missing from bunches sold in greengrocers.

Steamable, quichable, stir-fryable and perfect in salads, both these vegetables are cut-and-come-again crops, enthusiastically recycling grey-water and sunshine into fresh greens.

# Greens that store well

Root vegetables such as carrots, parsnips, onions, spuds, taro and sweet potato (both the white-fleshed purple-skinned variety, and the orange-fleshed **kumera**) are well known for their longevity in storage. They are best kept hanging in nets. Special plastic bags are available from supermarkets for the long-term storage of such vegetables. I believe these are very successful at extending the fresh characteristics, but at what chemical expense?

By far the best 'keeper' of all is the tuber from the yam bean (*Pachyrrhizus erosus*). This white-fleshed vegetable can be grated into coleslaw, chopped into fruit salad or added to stir-fry dishes, and retains its crunch well beyond carrots. The yam bean shoots readily, sending out vines like the kumera, however the leaves, flowers and bean pods of the yam bean plant are not edible as they contain rotenone, a potent insecticide.

Dates are essential stores for barefoot rovers. Deeply revered by Middle Eastern cultures as the 'Bread of the Desert', dates are bursting with food value: carbohydrates, fat and protein; vitamins A, B, D and G; iron, magnesium, potassium, phosphorous, calcium and copper. They also taste so good!

Prunes, currants and raisins deserve a lot of respect also, and store well long term without refrigeration.

Apart from dried fruits, the best fruits to store are whole watermelon, Granny Smith apples, and limes and lemons. Citrus fruit can be coated in Vaseline, as can eggs, to keep the airborne spoilers out. Whole coconuts are legendary for their keeping qualities, while the antiseptic properties of coconut milk have recently been recognised by Western medicine.

Knobs of fresh ginger and cloves of garlic can be stored well submerged in oil, such as peanut oil, in a jar. This prevents spoilers from reaching the air needed for them to multiply.

# Wild food

Old tamarind trees found along Australia's north coast stand as lasting evidence of the sites where Macassan trepangers salted, smoked and dried their catch hundreds of years ago, to carry it safely home by sailing ship without refrigeration. Tamarind leaves and flowers can be added sparsely to salads as one might add thyme. Tamarind seeds are edible after roasting. The pulp surrounding the seeds is familiar to cooks as a sour flavouring agent. It is also reputed to be a mild laxative.

Pipe dreaming, I am enticed to believe that boab trees and their edible nuts were introduced from darkest Africa by the people who etched the so-called Bradshaw figures into Kimberley cave walls significantly earlier than other Aboriginal art in the region. Boab nuts would be easily stowed for a long sea voyage. Green nuts can be roasted in their shell; the roasted pulp is then sweetened and eaten like stewed apple. One average-sized nut is ample for one serving.

Perhaps Chinese water chestnuts were introduced by seafarers centuries ago. Certainly these delicious chestnuts have escaped into waterways and thrive in profusion above the saltwater reaches where their dark green, hollow reed stems are easily recognisable. They are feral exotics, and share their habitat with the big snappy handbags — crocodiles.

Old graveyards, abandoned settlements, old lugger camps and stockyard camp sites and other such neglected places are often a good source of 'escaped' food-plants. Rosehips, limes and lemons, chilies, and sometimes pomegranates thrive in such places, as do **rosellas** (*Hibiscus sabdariffa*), which are in truth a native shrub of South Africa. The fruit of the rosella is passed off in posh restaurants as 'bush food' and sold for three times the price of a kilo of fillet steak, yet they grow wild along the road to the tip in Broome and through the Dampier peninsula. Frequently described as similar in flavour to cranberry, rosellas make beautiful ruby-red jam, excellent cordial spiced with cardamom, and, when eaten raw, make a very tart accompaniment for raw oysters. They can also be tossed in salads and included dried in dukkah.

Marsden Hordern in *King of the Australian Coast* cites records of Philip King's 1818 coastal survey aboard the *Mermaid* which describe how his team planted seeds in pockets of rich dark soil along the coast of Arnhem Land. Their list includes:

*peach stones, apricots, lemon seeds, Marrowfat peas, long podded peas, scarlet runners, Large Hornd Carrots, parsley, celery, parsnips, spinach, onions, cauliflower, turnips, cabbage, broad beans, tobacco, sweet and everlasting peas, and Spanish Broom.*

Wherever I venture ashore I am always hoping to discover a little grove of apricot trees!

# Wild bush tucker

Publications devoted to the identification of wild bush tucker are readily available, though barefoot rovers need to understand how scant the yields are, and how unpredictable the seasons. *Bush Tucker Identikit*, compiled by Glenn Wightman and Milton Andrews, lists some of the common native food plants of the Top End. The area covered extends from Broome to Weipa on the coast, and inland to Halls Creek and Tennant Creek. Colour photos and lots of information on habitat and uses make this a valuable resource book for barefoot rovers.

## Seaweeds

Some wild foods, such as nardoo seeds and the fruit of the burrawong palm, need to be treated in special ways to leach out toxins. Seaweeds, on the other hand, include a huge variety of plants edible straight from the water. It should be obvious that the best time to collect seaweeds in areas of extreme tidal ranges is at low tide. Kelp does not need to have been dried and powdered and sold through a health food store to taste good in your soup or stew or fish pie.

Most seaweeds I have tried don't lose their colour in cooking. They don't lose their flavour either, or their fierce cellophane or indiarubber texture! A very small number of seaweeds are poisonous. Those to be avoided are identified in elaborate books devoted to the subject of seaweeds, usually with detailed descriptions and photographs. For your own peace of mind, do some research before you set sail into a particular area, or stick to the abundant and well-known edible varieties such as kelp and sea-lettuce.

## Green cuisine

Shipboard greens can be as simple as a salad of strips of carrot or yam bean bulb, raisins, dates, chopped nuts and chopped apple, all doused in lime juice.

Use small pawpaw cut in half lengthwise as edible boats in which to serve coleslaw, cold fish, rice salad, chunks of cheese, kang kong, mayonnaise – anything.

# Potato Salad

This seems an appropriate place for the following recipe, a family 'secret' prepared every Christmas by old Uncle Hans.

**120g (4oz) chopped onion**

**$^1/_2$ cup fish stock**

**4 tablespoons olive oil**

**1 tablespoon white wine vinegar**

**$1^1/_2$ teaspoons Dijon mustard**

**$1^1/_2$ teaspoons salt**

**1 teaspoon black pepper**

**3 teaspoons lemon or lime juice**

**1 kg (2 lbs) potatoes, steamed, cooled and cubed**

Mix together in a saucepan all the ingredients except the lemon or lime juice and potatoes. Poach gently until the onion is translucent. Take it off the fire, cool, and add lemon or lime juice. Pour this dressing over the potatoes and coat evenly. To add a green dimension, finely chopped kang kong can be stirred in just before serving.

# Pickled Cabbage

Eaten cold in salads and sandwiches, home-pickled cabbage is another faithful stand-by for the provision of green value in a shipboard diet. This is a cinch to make, and works just as well for green cabbage as the traditional red. See page 66 for the recipe.

# Fish

With just a little more than the most basic knowledge of fishing, seafood can be relied upon as a constant and predictable source of fresh food for the barefoot rover cruising north of 18°S in Australian waters.

A dedicated angler is someone who has learnt to understand life from a piscine point of view. Why are fish found in certain habitats? Where and when do they forage and what do they prefer? In waters literally teeming with bait-fish it is futile to offer anything less tempting as bait. After all, if someone offered the angler a choice between a dish of yesterday's refried bubble-and-squeak or today's lobster thermidor, freshly cooked, what would the angler choose?

There are many theories about why these waters are so teeming with fish. The pearling industry operates to the exclusion of the trawling industry, for instance. But above all, the huge volume of water shifted daily in the tidal patterns means abundant nourishment for all aquatic creatures. Tidal ranges of nine metres (thirty feet) are commonplace. Catching top quality large table fish such as coral trout, red emperor, bluebone and barramundi is too easy, but in the galley the question explodes: What am I going to do with all this fish?!

The answer is found in various techniques of preserving, using uncomplicated traditional methods. The elements of barefoot fish preservation are: fresh fish and scrupulously clean utensils combined with agents such as salt, vinegar, smoke and spices.

On a boat without refrigeration, my advice is this: eat fresh fish straight out of the ocean, raw if you like, but go hungry rather than cook and eat fish if there is any doubt at all as to its freshness and palatability.

In the Central Pacific islands where I lived in the 1960s, the islanders ate first the fish liver, the heart and stomach, then good-naturedly vied for the chance to eat the eyes (a great delicacy). It makes sense to eat these morsels first, as they are more likely to be the first to succumb to nasty bacteria in the inevitable process of breakdown and putrefaction.

## Preserving fish

If, as so often happens, you catch a trophy-sized bluebone, take it ashore and cook it in a ground oven but can't eat it all at one meal, how do you save it for the next meal without refrigeration? The answer is to leave the bones for the hermit crabs and pack the cooked flesh loosely into glass jars and submerge it in a pickling liquid. I use home-brew sterilising powder to rinse out the jars first.

The recipes in this section will keep fish for a day or two; some will preserve it for as long as a week.

# Pickling Liquid

white peppercorns

mustard seed

dill seed

pimento

1 bay leaf

salt

chili (optional)

tamarind (optional)

cider vinegar

To prepare a pickling liquid to cover the fish, boil some white peppercorns, mustard and dill seed, pimento, a bay leaf and salt in a little water to extract the flavour; maybe chili and tamarind as well. Blend this with enough vinegar, such as cider vinegar, to flood the fish and submerge it.

For the next meal, lift the fish out of the pickle and coat each piece in olive oil, or yoghurt and dukkah, and eat it cold with doorstops of bread.

# Broome Susumi

Food in Broome reflects the way diverse cultures have been spliced together over generations. Many of the hard-hat divers of the early pearling luggers were Japanese and eventually there were many Japanese families in the town. Japanese purists may shudder at this recipe for Broome Susumi, but hungry crew relish it.

**boneless, skinless fillets of broadbar mackerel, bonito or northern bluefin tuna**

**fresh ginger**

**onion**

**chili**

**garlic**

**cider vinegar**

**honey**

**soy sauce (or fish sauce)**

**salt and pepper**

Lay raw pieces of fish, sliced to the thickness of banana skin, in a casserole dish. Add pieces of fresh ginger, onion, chili and garlic. Submerge all in a mixture of vinegar, honey, soy sauce and salt and pepper in the ratio of 4 parts vinegar to 1 part soy sauce, with a dash of honey. No further 'cooking' is necessary; the fish will be ready to eat the next day, and the next day, and the following day, though it must remain totally submerged until eaten.

# Finnish-Style Salted Fish (Gravlax)

**cooking salt**
**dark brown sugar**
**black pepper (or cayenne pepper)**
**fish**

Make a blend of cooking salt and dark brown sugar mixed in the proportion of 3 parts salt to 1 part sugar. Add black or cayenne pepper in whatever proportion you enjoy. Sprinkle a fine layer of this salt-mix over the base of a casserole dish. Next, carefully place a layer of fish pieces in, sliced no thicker than coarse orange peel, and not overlapping each other. Alternate the layers of salt-mix and fish pieces, finishing with a layer of salt-mix. Place a 'lid' on top, such as a bread-and-butter-plate, which rests on the fish, but not on the lip of the dish. Now place a weight such as a jam jar filled with lead fishing-sinkers on top of the plate. Overnight, the weight extracts excess moisture out of the fish, changing its texture, and a brine forms, in which the fish is submerged.

This gravlax mix is high in salt, which is why it seems to suit the tropics where salt is needed in the daily diet. Other mixes also work well and the proportions can be altered until a maximum of half sugar is reached. For the least-salt mix, shake together equal amounts of salt and white sugar with white pepper (and maybe 2 whole cloves and a bay leaf), and use the same technique to form a brine over your fish.

Fish preserved this way is especially enjoyed lifted out of the brine, chopped, and served with sweet beetroot and sour cream or yoghurt.

Another way to serve it is to lift it out of the brine, chop it finely, and toss it with fresh lime juice or vermouth, a chopped pickled lime and chopped kang kong. Simplest of all is to sprinkle dukkah onto the chopped fish and serve with hearth bread. This preserve keeps for a week, if you can keep it hidden from the skipper. The texture of the fish is determined by the amount of weight in the jam jar; too much weight results in a texture similar to shoe leather.

# Octopus

Octopus preserve keeps for three or four days, if there is any left over in the first place.

> **whole octopus**
> **vegetables (onion, carrot, fresh parsley, kang kong, tamarind pulp)**
> **freshly ground black pepper**
> **salt**
> **crushed garlic**
> **strong vinegar**

Put the occy (whole, but cleaned of its ink bag) and some vegetables, but no additional liquid, into a saucepan with a tight-fitting lid. Let it **'sweat'**, as the French say, which is to cook it slowly over a low flame with the saucepan tightly closed and retaining all the juices, until all is well cooked. Remove the flesh, chop it into forkable pieces and mix it with a liberal coating of freshly ground black pepper, salt and crushed garlic. Submerge all in strong vinegar. To serve it, lift pieces out of the vinegar and coat lightly with olive oil.

Alternatively, after sweating the occy, serve it hot, liberally coated with a sauce made from fried onion, tomato paste, tomatoes, pawpaw, black olives and capers.

# Fish Kibbeh

A Lebanese style dish, kibbeh is nearly the texture of bread.

> **325g pearled burghul (or cracked wheat)**
> **$\frac{1}{2}$ cup cold water (or fish stock)**
> **700g boneless raw fish**
> **2 large white onions**
> **cayenne and cinnamon**
> **salt and pepper to taste**
> **pine nuts (or fresh dill)**
> **oil**

Soak burghul in cold water or fish stock to cover for about 2 hours. Slice one onion and fry in oil until translucent, take off the fire and set aside. Mince together raw fish and second onion, mix in drained wheat and flavouring. Oil a lasagne dish, or similar shallow dish. Spread half the fish-mix in the dish, cover with fried onion and seasoning such as cayenne and cinnamon, or orange zest, pack the remaining fish mixture on top, level the surface and score it with the traditional diamond pattern. Sprinkle a little olive oil over the surface and bake in a moderate oven or lower for about 1 hour. When cooked it will start to shrink from the sides of the dish, but the length of time needed depends on how deep the mixture is in the dish.

# Soused Fish

    raw fish

    bay leaves (or dill seed, lime zest or tamarind)

    salt

    green peppercorns

    vinegar

    water (or cold tea)

Take pieces of raw fish, with or without skin and bone, and roll them like rollmops, or lay them flat in a casserole dish. Season them liberally with bay leaves, salt and green peppercorns. Now submerge them in a 3 : 1 mix of vinegar and water, or vinegar and cold tea. Poach them gently in the oven, and eat them cold tomorrow and the next day.

## Fish of the day

Because fish is so abundant in tropical latitudes, fish will frequently be on the menu. The simplest way to cook fish and probably the method that preserves the most food value is to steam it. The steaming water can be sea water. A steamer does not need to be a specially designed or beautiful fish kettle to work. All that is needed is some sort of device that will allow water to boil while the steam generated cooks the fish on a rack above. A lid trapping the steam makes it all more efficient.

*When frying fish, first coat the pieces in a light dusting of oatmeal, not wheat flour just for a change.*

# Fish-head Stock

Stock is any liquid tastier than plain water. On a boat there are always lots of trimmings from fish-cleaning that can be usefully included in stock, but seldom many vegetables. Good fish stock can be made from fish heads and trimmings and scraps such as carrot skins, spud skins, onion skins — anything that's not 'off' but surplus. Prepare the stock by boiling all the ingredients long enough to extract the flavour; strain and reserve liquid.

# Fish-head Soup

> any edible fish (bluebone is excellent)
>
> onion
>
> garlic
>
> ginger
>
> celery seed
>
> plain flour
>
> Squid Brand fish sauce
>
> pepper (or chili for extra zing)

pot-posy of fresh herbs (optional)

salt (optional)

Two-thirds fill your pressure cooker with the head and backbone, fins and skin (with or without scales) of the fish. Fill your cooker one-third with water and cook under pressure for 20 minutes.

When all has cooled sufficiently, drain and reserve the stock, and separate the best of the flesh from the bones. Fry some onion, garlic, ginger and celery seed; make a roux with a little plain flour; add a splash of fish sauce; add the soup stock and selected pieces of flesh and return it to the boil, stirring it to cook the flour and thicken the texture. Add pepper or chili or a pot-posy of fresh herbs, and salt if needed, and serve with doorstops of bread.

# Smoked Fish

raw mackerel tuna, free of bones or skin

salt

pinch citric acid

tamarind

Mackerel tuna is scorned by most people as a table fish, yet it smokes into a mouthwatering delicacy. First select pieces of raw fish, uniformly proportioned, say 10 cm long and 10 mm thick. Soak these for at least 1 hour in a solution of water, salt, a pinch of citric acid and a dash of tamarind.

Now you need to rig up a smoke-box somewhere, out on deck at anchor, or on shore. My smoke-box is made up of a metho burner from a Swedish camping stove, which heats a tin tray, on which smoke wood shavings and raw sugar, above which rests the fish on a metal grill, all of which is contained in a tin box roughly 30 cm square and 45 cm long. The metho burns for about 15 minutes; the smoke and heat circulate for about 20 minutes, after which the fish is ready to eat, today. This kind of smoking is for flavour; it's not a preservative measure. Any leftovers should be submerged in oil and eaten the next morning.

It was Peter Carman and Jenny Jeffery, aboard *Jarlem* out of Fremantle, who first persuaded me to use raw sugar as smoking fuel. Mullet is their favourite choice of fish to smoke; tiny slimy mackerel, heads and all, is mine.

# Tarawa Fish

The Kiribati islanders prepared Tarawa fish for us. Effortlessly trolling a lure astern a moving yacht frequently yields a Spanish mackerel. The average size of such a catch is probably around 9 kilos, yielding roughly 4 kilos of boneless, skinless meat.

The first time I tasted this recipe, Bauro of Nikunau Island in the Central Pacific had triumphantly brought ashore a marlin caught on a handline out of his 6-foot outrigger canoe! What a battle! That really is traditional fishing and deserves the greatest respect. Nothing was wasted from this catch. Bauro shyly gave the greatest delicacy, the eyes, to his treasured wife Nei Angea and she accepted them as a bounteous gift. Most of the dark meat was communally prepared as in the following recipe.

> **fresh fish, free of skin and bone**
> **limejuice (or limejuice and cider vinegar)**
> **raw onion, finely sliced (1 large onion per kilo of fish)**
> **salt and pepper**
> **fresh coconut cream (1 cup per kilo of fish)**

Cut the fish into 2.5-cm cubes. Marinate this in a mixture of limejuice and raw onion, salt and pepper (if your supply of limejuice is not enough to submerge the fish, augment it with cider vinegar). When the limejuice has reached the centre of the fish (easily recognised by a change in colour in the flesh) take the fish out of the juice and serve it, liberally coated with fresh coconut cream. This is ready to eat today and tomorrow, no further 'cooking' necessary.

# Fish Pie

Granny Smith apples, green and hard and tart, are ideal for this classic pie. I have also used delicious crabapples of a variety the size of ping-pong balls, grown as ornamentals. Proportions can be half fish and half onions-and-apples. Usually it will be more convenient to make it more than half fish because of the abundance of fish and paucity of apples and onions. Half a cup of stock is enough because a lot of juice will flow out of the other ingredients as it all cooks.

> **short pastry**
> **fillets of fish (e.g. Spanish mackerel)**
> **sliced apples**
> **sliced onions**
> **$\frac{1}{2}$ cup salted fish stock (or water and fish sauce)**

Line a greased pie dish with short pastry. Using fillets of fish sliced thinly, fill the dish with alternating layers of fish, sliced apple and sliced onion. Add fish stock and close the pie with a pastry lid. Cut holes in the lid to allow steam to escape as it cooks, and put it in a hot oven for 15 minutes. Reduce the heat to moderate and continue cooking for a further 20 minutes.
Eat it hot or cold.

# Fish Toes

Supermarket frozen fish fingers are made of an unidentifiable white substance that looks suspiciously pre-masticated. Fish Toes are far more down to earth because they are homemade. Cruising children gobble Fish Toes with relish, especially when they've made them themselves. The concoction should be at least fifty per cent fish.

> **cooked fish, free from bones**
>
> **mashed potato**
>
> **breadcrumbs (optional)**
>
> **raw onion, finely chopped**
>
> **celery seed**
>
> **dill or dill seed**
>
> **thyme**
>
> **cayenne**
>
> **Squid Brand fish sauce**
>
> **limejuice or tamarind**
>
> **1 egg**
>
> **salt and pepper**
>
> **oatmeal (or flour)**

Take a quantity of cooked fish, free from bones. It can be the leftovers from fish-head soup stock, or from a whole baked fish, or steamed or fried fish. Mix it with an equal quantity of mashed potato (or mashed potato combined with breadcrumbs). Now start adding flavour — finely chopped raw onion, celery seed, dill or dill seed, thyme, cayenne, fish sauce, limejuice or tamarind. A fresh egg will bind it together well. Mix it thoroughly, using your hands, and don't forget the salt and pepper. At this point a rest of an hour or two will help develop full flavour, but is not essential.

Form the mixture into 'toes' and coat each one in oatmeal or flour before shallow-frying in good fat.

Alternatively, spread it into a sponge cake tin, which has been greased and 'lined' with a light coating of polenta, and bake it in the Dutch oven at a moderate temperature. Cut it into 'toes' to serve as finger food.

# Taramasalata

The Greeks, as one would expect, are expert seafood cooks, and taramasalata — a dip or spread based on **fish roe**, the culinary name for fish eggs — is a well-loved recipe of Greek cuisine. Fish milt (sperm) may also be used. (Fish roe varies in size according to maturity and species, and the flavour also varies, but all are edible. Roe can be cooked in batter or breadcrumbs, fried or grilled, or added to soups, pies and casseroles.) This recipe for taramasalata is in the style of Greek cookery, at least.

> **120g stale breadcrumbs**
>
> **60g raw fish roe from a large catfish (very rich dark yellow roe) or the milt from**
>    **Spanish mackerel, or both**
>
> **$^1/_2$ cup olive oil**
>
> **1 tablespoon thin tamarind juice for a lemon flavour (or limejuice)**
>
> **1 white onion, minced**

Moisten the breadcrumbs with cold water and allow several minutes for them to become saturated. Beat together with the roe and/or milt. Gradually beat in olive oil, tamarind or lime juice and minced onion. Add pepper and salt and the dish is ready. No further 'cooking' is necessary. Serve it spread on bread or toast, or use it to combine ingredients in a potato salad or leftover cooked fish. Don't expect it to keep well without refrigeration; eat it all the day the fish is caught.

# Batarekh

An Egyptian dish, batarekh treats fish roe in a special way. For this, the roe needs to be intact, retained in their natural membranous sack without punctures or tears. The humble catfish, so despised by anglers, so unkindly underrated, provides an exquisite roe for this recipe.

> **intact, raw roe**
>
> **cooking salt**
>
> **spices (chili, cayenne, cumin and white pepper)**

Liberally coat the roe with cooking salt. The salt may be jazzed up with barefoot roving preservatives: spices such as chili, cayenne, cumin and white pepper. Each roe is left standing on absorbent paper. As the salt draws the moisture out of the roe they must be turned, re-salted and the paper changed. This happens fastest in a shady place where warm dry air is blowing across the roe. Gradually the moisture content is extracted and the skin hardens. The length of time needed depends on the temperature and humidity, but should only take a few days. They are ready when they look desiccated and have a coarse skin but are still pliant.

This treatment concentrates the marine flavour and provides a salty delicacy to slice and serve on bread. Olive oil or lemon juice may be added as a dressing. For the passionate epicure they are an exquisite delight, well worth the time and tedium involved in their preparation.

# Calamari

In the 1980s we met the 130-year-old little-ship *Dresden*, the lady in the life of Richard Pennyfather. Measuring 40' overall, 37' on deck, 35' waterline length, with a tiny 8'2" beam and 4'6" draft, she carries 9 tons of lead ballast and all up boasts 18.5 tons! Her mizzen mast had been carried away in a collision, and made me ponder on the meaning of the term 'mizzen': it was mizzen all right, missin' altogether. Her massively built teak hull gave out the delicious aroma of beeswax and wood turps.

*Dresden* also gave us the delicious aroma of fried calamari (squid or cuttlefish).

> **calamari pieces**
>
> **milk**
>
> **1 teaspoon cultured sour cream (optional)**
>
> **flour**
>
> **egg, lightly beaten**
>
> **desiccated coconut**
>
> **ghee**

Steep calamari pieces in milk (and sour cream if desired — the lactic acid tenderises the flesh). Roll in flour, then egg, then desiccated coconut. Shallow-fry gently in ghee. Best served with a sweet-sour sauce.

# Squid with Fresh Herbs

1 tablespoon tamarind pulp, soaked and sieved

3 tablespoons Squid Brand fish sauce

3 tablespoons fresh limejuice

1 tablespoon sugar

7 cloves garlic, minced

1 red onion, sliced

2 red chilies, chopped

$1/2$ cup chopped mint and coriander (or other fresh herbs)

$1/2$ cup chopped roasted peanuts

1 kg cleaned squid, cut into bite-sized morsels

stock of lime zest, lemongrass and salt

Prepare the dressing by blending together all the ingredients except the squid, the stock ingredients, the fresh herbs and the peanuts, and set aside to develop full flavour.

In a saucepan of boiling water make a tasty stock with the zest, lemongrass and salt. When it is at a rollicking boil add the squid pieces, cooking them quickly just until they turn opaque. Lift them out of the stock onto a plate. When drained, add them to the dressing and toss well. Lastly, add the green herbs and sprinkle the roasted peanuts over the top.

# Stuffed Squid

This recipe is from a Vietnamese friend, The Ahn, champion angler and crabber.

      30g cellophane noodles

      1$\frac{1}{2}$ tablespoons dried tree ear mushrooms

      6 medium whole squid with tentacles (about 1 kg)

      1 small Spanish onion finely chopped

      2 teaspoons cracked black pepper

      2 tablespoons Squid Brand fish sauce

      $\frac{1}{4}$ cup peanut oil

      2 small tomatoes, sliced

      3 large spring onions, greens only, cut into 5-cm lengths

Soak the noodles in cold water or cold fish stock until pliable, about 5 minutes; drain, cut into small lengths and set aside.

Soak the mushrooms in hot water, or hot fish stock until soft, about 2 minutes; drain, and chop coarsely. Set aside.

Remove the tentacles and little side 'wings' (or rudders) from the squid. Finely chop these trimmings and set aside in a large bowl. Remove and discard the cartilage and ink sack. Rinse the squid well. Make a small incision just below the closed end of the squid helmet to prevent bursting during cooking.

To the bowl of chopped tentacles and wings, add the noodles, mushrooms, onion, pepper and all but 2 teaspoons of the fish sauce. Mix well, and fill each helmet with the stuffing.

Shallow-fry the squid in hot peanut oil, then remove them to a serving dish.

Pour off excess oil from the pan, then add tomatoes and the remaining fish sauce, and simmer until the tomatoes are soft and mushy. Remove from the heat and stir in the spring onion greens. Pour over the squid and serve hot, with coriander chili sauce as an extra indulgence.

# Cherabin

Cherabin (*Macrobrachium rosenbergii*) are the local tropical prawns found in tidal and freshwater reaches of rivers, creeks and billabongs. They can be enticed to congregate in clusters by dropping chicken pellets or bread into shallow water. A circular cast-net is then thrown over them to trap them. Cook them like crabs by boiling in a tasty stock. Don't crowd the pot. Measure the cooking time from when the water returns to the boil. They need only minutes to cook and rise to the surface when done. Five minutes should be the maximum time needed. Eat them the day they are caught.

# Giant Clams

These enormous bivalves are easily located in rock pools. However, before you calculate on harvesting one for the pot, understand that the only really edible portion is the actual muscle. Is it worth sacrificing the whole creature for such a relatively small amount of food?

# Juringa Muddies

If you don't claim Indigenous bloodlines, but want to eat mud crabs (*Scylla paramamosain*), you first need to find out about local regulations relating to female crabs. Some states ban the taking of females altogether. Females have a distinctly broader abdominal flap, or 'apron'; males have a narrow, pointed abdominal flap.

Muddies are one of the most delicious foods around, as rich in flavour as lobster. Muddies keep — alive — for many days. Once cooked, they should be eaten as soon as possible because bacteria love them too.

Muddies can be cooked on the coals of a shore fire, or on a barbecue plate. Many people declare this method retains the most concentrated flavour. Another way is to steam crabs by standing the crab on a wire rack above boiling water in the pressure cooker. I prefer to simmer them in a tasty stock.

> **mud crabs**
> **salted water (sea water is fine)**
> **fresh ginger**
> **fresh garlic**
> **tamarind**
> **peppercorns**
> **oregano**
> **dark brown sugar**
> **malt vinegar**

Simmer the muddies gently in a stock of salted water and ginger, garlic, tamarind, peppercorns, oregano and a little dark brown sugar and malt vinegar. Boil the stock first, for several minutes, to develop the flavour in the water, then add the crab. Five minutes at boiling point should be long enough for even the largest crab. Don't overcrowd the pot; it's better to cook crabs one at a time.

Blue swimmer crabs (*Portunus pelagicus*) can be cooked this way too.

# Trepang

Also called sea cucumber and beche-de-mer, trepang are aquatic creatures known to marine biologists as holothurians and to children as sea slugs. By whatever name, there are over 650 species identified; of those, the most sought after for culinary purposes are, according to the Western Australian Fisheries Department:

**white teatfish (*Microthele fuscogilva*)**

**black teatfish (*Microthele nobilis*)**

**sandfish (*Metriatyla scabra*)**

**blackfish (*Actinopyga* sp.)**

**deepwater redfish (*Actinopyga echinites*)**

**prickly redfish (*Thelenota ananas*)**

**surf redfish (*Actinopyga mauritiana*)**

A good marine biology reference book may help identify them with descriptions of colour, size, shape, habitat etc. but is extremely unlikely to give information about whether or not they are edible or how to prepare them.

From those I have tried so far — in soups, stir-fries, pickled or soused — the big white teatfish is definitely the tastiest. Equally definitely, the least tasty is the most common black fish.

Trepang are a culinary delicacy among ethnic Chinese in particular, and among Asians generally. They may be found at the marketplace boiled, gutted, salted, dried, smoked and trussed. This last process is not essential and its primary function is the convenience of transportation and stowage in vessels without refrigeration.

There is no sporting chance involved in capturing trepang. Found in tidal pools and along stretches of sandy bottom between reefs close to the shore, they are as easy to collect as seashells along the beach. In water deeper than convenient for gathering, the technique used is to spear them with a weighted spear retrieved by a length of fishing line.

It seems the trepang's only method of defence is to spew white threads which are mildly irritating to the skin. Vinegar adequately counters the irritation.

This local food source is not exactly one for which we have an insatiable appetite, but it's comforting to know that holothurians are edible. What's more, they need scant preparation from the galley.

## Preparing trepang

Place the live trepang into fresh water for half a minute. Once removed from the fresh water, they obligingly regurgitate almost all of their threads, along with the sand and sludge in their gut. Slit them lengthwise and finish the job.

Indonesians prepare trepang for the table by merely slitting them, cleaning out the intestine, scraping the slime off the flesh, then slicing them into strips 10 mm wide, steeping the slices in vinegar for three minutes and eating them. No further 'cooking' is needed.

My mother Lilian Burbury's recipe for trepang soup, dated 1927, describes slitting the trepang and cleaning out the gut, then boiling it in a large volume of water, lifting out the froth and scum as it forms on the surface. After this pre-cooking the flesh is ready to be chopped and included in a seafood soup. The parboiled flesh can also be used in stir-fry dishes.

# Trepang and Occy

**trepang**

**octopus**

**garlic**

**ginger**

**vinegar**

**dressing of oil, vinegar and mustard (or taramasalata)**

Chop the trepang and octopus. Parboil the trepang flesh and then fry it with garlic and ginger. Prepare the octopus in the same way, then submerge both in vinegar. To serve, lift out of the vinegar and coat it with a dressing of oil, vinegar and mustard, or toss it into taramasalata.

# Aku Ankka Sea Cucumber

Erja Vasumaki, aboard the intrepid *Aku Ankka*, sent me her trepang recipe postmarked Kuching in October 1999.

**trepang**

**butter**

**garlic**

*You want my favourite sea-cucumber recipe! These are the ones we ate back in the Pacific North West, large 30-50 cm ones. Open each cucumber lengthwise. With a sharp knife carefully 'lift off' the long strips of muscle (I think it's 6 of them) off its slimy thick skin. Fry these in a bit of butter and garlic for about 30 seconds. Very good! You need several for a meal. Bit of work but they're superb like this.*

# Painted Crayfish

Painted crayfish (*Panulirus versicolor*) also are rarely troubled by commercial operators, not only because they maintain a vegetarian diet and therefore resist walking into cray pots baited with meat, but because their flavour is second rate compared with other crayfish.

Painted crays, like trepang, need only to be lifted out of their habitat. They are well camouflaged among coral, and are one of the most delicately and exquisitely decorated of all tropical sea creatures. To counter the bitter element in their natural flavour the chef must include two rather unexpected ingredients: a piece of mace and a teaspoon of vanilla extract per cray. Sounds unlikely? Try it! It really does the trick.

# Meat

Foreign cruising boats visiting Australian shores need to be aware that only Indigenous Australians are allowed to kill native species such as dugong, turtle, goanna, pied geese, brush turkey and brolga, bilbies, possums, koalas and parrots.

There does, however, remain the age-old right of castaways to eat anything to maintain life and limb — although old records of survival at sea in open lifeboats reveal again and again that it is possible to live for many days without food, but impossible to survive long without water.

I am ridiculously sentimental about dugong (perhaps the mermaids of folklore) and turtle; I would have to be desperately hungry (and by then probably too weak to act) before I could ever decide to kill one.

Feral camel, donkey, goat, pig and horse all thrive in the Top End, and are all meats I have eaten. A Vietnamese friend can't understand how there can be feral cats and dogs in Australia when cats and dogs make such good food. On the Indonesian island of Babar, dog meat is a special delicacy at wedding feasts.

Yet another source of introduced meat in Australia is guinea fowl, a bird of the plains country of Africa. Guinea fowl are roughly the size of domestic fowl but are more active, running in dithering groups and quickly taking wing if disturbed, only to glide back to ground after a short distance. They are constantly calling to each other, the male with a very repetitive call; the female with a two-note call which distinctly says 'come back, come back'.

Guinea fowl feathers are grey speckled with white, or khaki and dark brown, and the head carries a distinctive red helmet and red wattles on both male and female. A mature bird weighs about one and a half kilos. The meat is superb — succulent and gamy, pale-coloured on the breast and darker on the legs. Cook it with juniper berries and cinnamon in a closed Dutch oven, long and slow, retaining all the juices.

Guinea fowl eggs are small compared to those of domestic fowl, and have a more distinct point at one end. Their colour is ivory, and they are found in communal nests on the ground.

If you wish to reduce the wild game flavour of meat, such as pied geese, use cinnamon in the recipe when cooking the meat. If you wish to increase the flavour of bland meat, to make it more 'gamy', add Angostura Bitters in the cooking.

A mash of the leaves & fruit of pawpaw, spread over meat as a marinade, will tenderise it overnight.

# Pressure cooker meat preservation

If you slaughter a pig, even a small pig, the only thing you can't eat is the squeal. You will have a good supply of the best sausage skins available (the small intestine casing); you will also have on your hands a large quantity of meat to store. When planning to carry any kind of meat as stores without refrigeration, the best solution is to do as Dave Legge did aboard the Wharram cat *Juringa*: cook it simply and bottle it in preserving jars in the pressure cooker. Jars and rings must be in tip-top condition, and meat must be thoroughly cooked before it goes into the jars.

Pack the meat in the jars, leaving about 20 mm headroom. Cover the meat with vegetable or meat stock or salted water (half a teaspoon of salt to a pint jar). Wipe jar rims carefully and check rings and clips, then cook in the pressure cooker at 10 lbs of pressure or higher. Pint jars (600 ml) need about 75 minutes; quart jars (about 1000 ml) about 90 minutes.

To prepare this preserved meat for the table, make a tasty gravy or curry sauce and heat the meat in it to serve.

The McDonald family — Bernie, Sue and Ruth — aboard the steel ketch *New Liver Bird* (expertly handcrafted out of a water tank), have been preserving meat in this way since leaving North Wales in the 1980s. They handed on the skill to Dave Legge in the way many such skills are shared, compared and endlessly discussed among the diverse fraternity of cruisers.

# Pressure Cooker Irish Stew

For most cooks Irish Stew is as basic as boiling water, but there is one special technique for cooking it in a pressure cooker. The thickening is not added until last. Chuck steak is a suitable meat, and there is no need to extract the fat from the lean.

> **2 tablespoons oil or fat**
>
> **1 kilo meat, roughly cubed**
>
> **4 cups cubed vegetables (e.g. carrots, turnips, yam bean)**
>
> **2 cups cubed potato**
>
> **1 onion, sliced**
>
> **2 cups water with 1 beef stock cube dissolved**
>
> **1 tablespoon arrowroot (mix to a thin paste with water)**
>
> **salt and pepper**

Heat the oil in the bottom of the pressure cooker and fry the meat at a high temperature, stirring it off the bottom and browning all sides. Add all the vegetables and stir well to heat fairly evenly. Add the water and stir to lift off any browning stuck to the bottom of the cooker. Close the cooker, seal it and bring it to pressure. Hold it at pressure for about 40 minutes then take the cooker off the fire. As soon as the pressure has dropped, open the lid and stir the arrowroot paste into the stock in the pot. It will thicken as gravy without needing to boil. Add salt and pepper last.

# Jumbuck Pie

This is an old family favourite, just as good made with toothless old mutton as with billy-goat or roo meat.

> 1 kilo lean meat
>
> 1 onion, chopped
>
> 1 glass red wine
>
> 3 or 4 salted anchovies
>
> 1 dessertspoon capers
>
> 30g butter (or good fat)
>
> 30g plain flour
>
> suet pastry

Cut the meat into forkable pieces. With a very little fat and a chopped onion, put the meat in a tightly lidded casserole dish or saucepan and let it 'sweat', as the French say — cooking it very slowly and retaining all the juices. The tougher the meat the longer and slower it needs to cook.

When the meat is cooked, take it off the fire and drain off the juice. Add a glass of red wine to the juice, and in this rich stock poach the anchovies and capers.

In a separate saucepan, melt the butter and make a roux with the flour. Blend in the stock to boil into gravy. Add salt and pepper if necessary. Pour the gravy over the meat in the casserole dish and top with a lid of suet pastry, leaving a hole for steam to escape. Bake the pie in a hot oven until the pastry is cooked, probably about 20 minutes.

# Terrapin

I include the following details on terrapin — the long-necked land-based tortoise — from my mother's handwritten recipe book, since turtle can be cooked in the same way. This is better than wasting it. Too many people catch turtle and then don't know how much is edible. I don't want to encourage the killing of turtles in Australian waters, but it is legal in many countries.

*To boil Terrapin: Plunge into boiling water. Boil 5 minutes. Remove from water. Rub skin off feet and tail with a rough towel. Pull off head with a skewer, and rub off the skin. Place in a saucepan. Add a stick of celery and two slices each of carrot and onion. Simmer until the meat is tender, 35-40 minutes. Remove from the water. Cool. Draw nails from feet. Cut under-shell quite close to upper shell and remove. Empty top shell and carefully remove and throw away the gall-bladder, thick heavy part of the intestines, and sand-bags. Now finish off in one of the following ways, remembering that the small intestine and liver are edible.*

*Savoy Terrapin: 1 terrapin, 1 cup cream, 2 eggs, 2 tablespoons sherry or milk, 1 tablespoon butter, ditto flour, half cup chopped mushrooms, salt and cayenne. Melt butter in a saucepan, stir in the flour and, when frothy, slowly stir in cream. Bring to boiling point. Stir in terrapin meat with chopped bones and intestines, broken up liver, Terrapin eggs and mushrooms. Season with salt and cayenne. When ready to serve, stir in lightly beaten eggs and wine or milk. Stir until thickened.*

# Curries

Curries are the traditional food of hot countries such as India. Not every home in India boasts a fridge, but I think it's fair to say every home enjoys curry, with or without meat. I think there's a connection here that is not always obvious to western eyes — the spices traditionally blended for curry paste have at least some power of preservation or antibacterial properties. Their powerful and exhilarating flavour is just a bonus. Blends of curry spices will even mask the too-strong flavour of stale meat or fish. Allowing meat or fish to 'sudder' (cook at just below boiling point) for 20 minutes ensures bacteria are destroyed.

# Spices

| | |
|---|---|
| ginger | mustard seed |
| garlic | pepper |
| chili | star-anise |
| cumin | celery seed |
| coriander seed | cardamom |
| turmeric | mace |
| cinnamon | nutmeg |

Ginger, garlic and chili are almost mandatory curry spices. Their strong flavours are balanced and enhanced by the colourful addition of masala, a condiment of roasted and ground spices blended with care. Masala offers enormous scope for the quirks and fancies of the cook. Obviously I like to venture further than a tin of commercial curry powder!

Spices should be purchased and stored in their whole form whenever possible. That way their best flavour is preserved. Even whole turmeric can be bought in shopping districts where curries are the norm. The difference in flavour is as distinct as the difference between dried powdered ginger and fresh ginger root.

Traditional Asian wok stir-fries demand the freshest of ingredients, but curries can tolerate ingredients past their prime. They benefit from long slow cooking, make good use of the cheapest cuts of meat from the butcher, and offer scope for improvisation — using up excess coconuts before crossing the state border, for instance.

Vindaloo curries use vinegar as the liquid in which the meat is cooked. The acid in the vinegar helps to tenderise really tough cuts. A moli curry has a coconut-milk or cream liquid base, and usually includes toasted mustard seed. An Indonesian moli is known as laksa, but does not use mustard.

# Concocting a Curry

Curries really suit a hot climate. Not only do they offer what I believe is natural protection against germs and bacteria, but the spices, especially the chili, promote natural refrigeration in the form of perspiration. Let it flow!

Begin by deciding which flavours you prefer, and in what proportions. Blending flavours and varying proportions offers huge scope for individual expression. A good result is often one where diners really enjoy the delicious flavour but can't quite distinguish exactly what's in it. Unusual inclusions such as juniper berries or star-anise can be a great success if used with subtlety. Mace adds depth to the basic favourite blend of cumin, coriander and turmeric.

When you make your own curry powder, like the garam masala recipe below, whole seeds are dry-roasted, or toasted, until they pop, then ground with the other spices in a pestle and mortar.

Dried fruit such as apricots, currants and raisins are excellent flavour surprises and will also absorb excess liquid. Letting the sauce stand while excess liquid is taken up by the dried fruit avoids the necessity of using extra cooking fuel to reduce the liquid by boiling.

# Garam Masala

An acceptable short-cut for the curry cook is to have a small supply of masala on hand. Garam masala is stocked in Asian groceries and on supermarket shelves, but homemade tastes best because it's fresher — and because you made it yourself. The recipe below gives the amount you would need for the Pork Vindaloo recipe that follows. If you want to have some extra on hand, double the quantities.

> 1 tablespoon coriander seed
>
> 1 dessertspoon cumin seed
>
> the seeds of 2 green cardamom pods (they should be black and sticky)
>
> 10 mm piece of cinnamon
>
> 3 cloves
>
> 3 black peppercorns
>
> 1 teaspoon ground turmeric
>
> knob of ginger
>
> 2 teaspoons chili powder (more or less)
>
> ½ teaspoon salt

Lightly dry-roast the coriander seeds until they pop, then the cumin. Crush them with the rest of the ingredients in the mortar.

# Pork Vindaloo

In this recipe the pork is marinated in vinegar for at least an hour, but longer if conditions allow. On board the cook must always be flexible. If the cook is piped up on deck to reef a sail — or take the helm while the skipper does some navigation, or help anchor, tie up or raft off, or just to attend to the radio when customs and coast watch call from an aircraft — then the cooking must wait. Conversely, if you are safely anchored somewhere and all is snug, then likely as not the crew are pacing the deck starving hungry, growling like lions at the galley hatch with dire threats if the cook doesn't hurry and feed them all. Because the vinegar is enriched with preservative spices, the meat can safely marinate overnight if the weather is not too hot.

> **750g pork**
>
> **apple cider vinegar**
>
> **2 tablespoons garam masala**
>
> **3 cloves garlic**
>
> **ghee**
>
> **1 teaspoon red or yellow mustard seed**

Roughly cube the pork and pierce each piece with a sail needle to help the spices saturate the meat. Wash the pork cubes in vinegar and discard the vinegar. Form a thin paste by adding a cup of vinegar to the masala. Rub the paste into the meat cubes and place them in a bowl. Submerge all in vinegar. Leave the meat to marinate for at least 1 hour.

Crush the garlic, heat some ghee and fry it gently. Add the mustard seeds and let them pop. Empty the bowl of pork into the pan, including all the juices, and simmer, or 'sudder', it gently until the meat is tender. Water should never be added to vindaloo.

Because this meat is virtually pickled by this process it will keep satisfactorily overnight, provided it stays submerged in vinegar or oil.

# Fish Moli

1 kg fish fillets

1 teaspoon arrowroot or rice flour

1 cup coconut cream

$1/2$ teaspoon dry-roasted cumin seed

1 piece of mace

1 teaspoon ground turmeric (or grated fresh turmeric)

2 cloves crushed garlic

1 sliced green chili

ghee for frying

1 teaspoon whole yellow mustard seed

2 sliced onions

limejuice

Carefully blend the arrowroot into the coconut cream. Grind the cumin seed and mace in the mortar. Add that to the coconut cream with the turmeric, garlic, chili and some salt. Heat some ghee in a pan and pop the mustard seed, add onions and let them cook gently until translucent. Add fish fillets to the pan and pour in the spiced cream. Simmer all gently — or 'sudder' as they say — until the fish is cooked. Dash in a few drops of limejuice just before serving.

See also Lima Bean Tuna Curry on page 128.

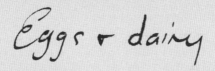

# Eggs & dairy

A truly fresh egg is a prize in any galley. I'll bet the head chef aboard the QEII would give her eye-teeth for a truly fresh egg. A truly fresh egg 'stands up' with vitality, and is essential to such culinary delights as mayonnaise, custard (needing yolks with vitality), omelettes and souffle (needing whites with vitality), to name just a few. Pavlova is the only dish that benefits from stale eggwhite.

In a permaculture egg production system, domestic fowls flourish. A handful of hens and one rooster browse and scratch from dawn to dusk, happily recycling unappetising forms of protein (ticks and spiders, maggots and mice) into neatly packaged glistening gems. Eggs contain more than protein, but it is the amount of protein consumed that determines the size of the egg. In a permaculture system the hen lays an egg a day in a nesting site of her choice, until she has a clutch of maybe fifteen eggs. Next, she goes broody and settles on the clutch to incubate them until they all hatch together, twenty days later. Simple arithmetic will tell you that the first egg laid is at least two weeks older than the last egg laid, yet though it has not been refrigerated, it is as fresh as the most recent egg laid and will hatch on the same day. This freshness is the rooster's natural contribution to the gem: the egg has been fertilised — it is viable.

The housing of hens in batteries for egg production is probably the most loathsome disgrace of all our twentieth-century lamentable food production travesties. Besides the suffering of the hens, battery eggs are never as vitally fresh as natural eggs because they are not fertilised. If you have never cooked with truly fresh eggs, find some and try them.

For some time now my most vivid pipedream has been to devise a way to carry live quail on deck! Fowl and pigs were carried as a matter of course by Flinders and King when they were charting this coastline in the nineteenth century.

If you are not fortunate enough to carry live fowl on board, and wish to preserve eggs to maintain a supply for some months, there are various techniques to follow. Obviously, the success of preservation relates directly to the quality and freshness of the eggs in the first place.

A simple test for freshness is to submerge the unbroken eggs in a large bowl of fresh water. A fresh egg lies on the bottom, a not-so-fresh-egg has one end rising up towards the surface, and a stale egg floats. This is because there is a pocket of air inside the shell, and as the egg turns rotten the amount of air increases.

There is absolutely no substitute for truly fresh eggs, so if you can't get them, it's better to avoid recipes that need eggs. However, as a very last resort, see page 46 for substitutes when you are desperate.

## Preserving uncooked eggs

To preserve uncooked eggs you need to stop air and bacteria from penetrating the shell. Waterglass (sodium silicate) was the common means of preserving eggs when I was a child. Fresh eggs were submerged in a solution of one part waterglass 'syrup' to eleven parts boiled and cooled water in an old milk bucket. The solution needs to be kept very still and is therefore not recommended for use aboard pitching and rolling cruisers! Furthermore, eggs held in this way need a temperature below 5°C, far from the climatic conditions north of 18°S.

Today, in the tropics, coating each egg with petroleum jelly (Vaseline) works well. However, as the weeks go by, you will need to inspect each egg before using it. Break an egg onto a saucer first; if it looks and smells all right go ahead and use it. In the Kimberley, eggs stored this way really only last about four or five weeks. In cooler temperatures they last eight weeks.

# Pickled Eggs

Eggs which are to be eaten hard boiled in salads or sandwiches can be boiled well in advance and preserved in spiced vinegar.

> **eggs**
>
> **strong (very acid) spiced vinegar (mustard seed, toasted cumin seed,**
> **dill seed, peppercorn)**

Cook the eggs, in their shells, in water held at just-boiling for at least 10 minutes. The eggs must be thoroughly hard boiled. Cool the eggs and peel them, and stack them in scrupulously clean, sterilised jars.

To flavour the vinegar, take a small quantity of vinegar, enough to cover the spice, and heat it with mustard, cumin and dill seed and peppercorns (or whatever else you fancy), holding it just below boiling point for three minutes to infuse the flavours. While it is still hot, pour this infusion over the eggs in the jars, and top up to the brim with cold unflavoured vinegar.

Tightly close the jars with lids that will not corrode from the acid in the vinegar. Glass coffee jars with a glass lid and plastic collar insert are ideal. Brimful and sealed with waterproof masking tape, they are a never-fail stand-by. Eggs prepared this way store well for easily four months.

# Salted Eggs

This method is described by A. Hepworth in the *Liklik Buk* from the Lae Information Centre in Papua New Guinea.

**Utensils: Kettle, glass jars, measuring cups.**

**Raw materials: chicken eggs with shell; coarse salt; plastic bag; muslin cloth.**

*Wash eggs very clean.*

*Prepare brine solution by boiling enough water to cover the eggs. Add salt by the handful and stir to dissolve it. Continue adding salt until the last addition will no longer dissolve. Saturation point is reached by adding about 2 cups salt to 1 cup water. Allow brine to cool.*

*Carefully pack eggs in wide-mouthed glass jar or ceramic container.*

*Pour cold brine solution over eggs. Weigh down with plate or cup to keep eggs from floating or use a sealed plastic bag filled with the brine solution.*

*Cover mouth of container with 2 or 3 layers of muslin cloth or any suitable cover. Keep in a cool dry place.*

*After 12 days, boil an egg and taste. If not salt enough for your taste, keep remaining eggs in the solution for one week longer.*

# Top End Mayonnaise

This mayonnaise can be prepared from preserved hard-boiled eggs.

     **1 egg**

     **salt and pepper**

     **mustard powder**

     **$^1/_2$ cup coconut cream**

     **vinegar**

Mash the hard-boiled yolk of an egg with salt, pepper and dry mustard powder. Mix in the coconut cream and add a splash of vinegar.

Pickled eggs can be cut in half lengthwise, the yolk turned into mayonnaise and then piled back into the whites. Sprinkle dukkah over the top, add some sprigs of kang kong and serve as an entree.

# Mayonnaise Francaise

A classic culinary triumph when prepared by hand. You will need:

>  2 fresh eggs (with the emphasis on fresh)
>
>  1 teaspoon mustard powder or 1 teaspoon unrefined honey
>
>  $^1/_2$ teaspoon salt
>
>  180 ml cold pressed virgin olive oil (no substitute!)
>
>  2 dessertspoons cider vinegar or limejuice

You will need a mixing bowl of around 5 cups (1–2 pint) capacity and some means of holding it steady while you beat the ingredients vigorously with a hand beater or whisk, or a table fork with long prongs. For instance, take another much larger bowl, a really heavy one, and wedge the smaller one inside it by packing a tea towel around it. Stand the larger bowl on a wet cloth.

Don't even dream of starting this if you are likely to be piped up on deck to help tack, or drop anchor, or take over the helm for a minute.

Separate the yolks and place them in the inner bowl. Add the mustard or honey and the salt. Blend this together well. Now comes the essential but tricky part of the procedure: the olive oil must be added a single drop at a time, while you keep beating. Once the mayonnaise starts to 'stand up' you may add the oil at a faster rate.

To control the flow of oil, dip a skewer into the bottle and hold it over the basin, letting the oil run down the skewer to drip into the mixture. Beat in each tiny drip very well before adding the next. You will be adequately rewarded by a thick, velvet soft, glorious emulsion, which will only just slide off the spoon.

Blend in the vinegar or lime juice last.

# Pavlova

A national dish of Australia named in honour of the Russian ballerina, Anna Pavlova, who danced so lightly on her pointes. Pavlova needs eggwhites and caster sugar combined in the ratio of 60g sugar for every eggwhite.

> **4 stale eggwhites**
>
> **pinch of cream of tartar**
>
> **1$^1/_2$ cups caster sugar**
>
> **1 teaspoon cider vinegar**
>
> **1 teaspoon vanilla essence**
>
> **1 dessertspoon arrowroot (cornflour is second best)**

Beat the eggwhites and cream of tartar to soft peaks; add the caster sugar gradually, while you continue beating. Beat it to a stiff meringue, then carefully fold in the cider vinegar, vanilla essence and arrowroot.

Grease a baking sheet and powder it with arrowroot; tip the mixture onto the sheet and shape it into a dinner-plate size with a raised wall mounded around the edge. Bake it in a very, very slow oven until the pale fawn crust is crisp. The inside should remain soft, like marshmallow. Traditionally, whipped cream is piled into the cold Pavlova, but galley-made yoghurt, sweetened with honey and loaded with fresh fruit like pawpaw, is just as good.

# Quirky Scrambled Eggs

For Tim aboard the Wharram cat *Quirky*, here is the secret of easy scrambled eggs. It takes only two ingredients:

> **eggs**
>
> **butter**

Begin by melting an amount of butter equal to half the volume of the eggs you mean to use. Break in the eggs and stir it along so it doesn't stick to the bottom of the pot. It will all go on cooking after you take it off the fire, so snatch it off early. If you managed to get the proportions correct it will leave the pot clean. If you skimped on the butter some of the egg will be cooked onto the bottom of the pot and stuck like glue. Practice makes perfect!

# Omelette Fingerfood

> **sippets**
>
> **eggs**
>
> **butter**

Fry sippets of bread in butter; when crisp, pour into the same pan and cook, with the sippets, an omelette batter — eggs that have been beaten vigorously until light and frothy. When it's done, roll it up, cut it in sections and hand it around as finger food. You can also make this with a basic pancake mixture.

# Pancakes

1 egg

1¼ cups milk

1 cup plain white flour

2 teaspoons melted butter

salt and pepper

Mix all together to form a thin-to-medium batter. It should cling to the spoon, coating it lightly. Allow the mixture to rest for 5 minutes to help the flour absorb the moisture. Fry in batches of a quarter cup at a time, on a warm-to-hot girdle, turning to brown both sides.

# Dairy

Milk aboard a cruiser will nearly always be powdered. In its powdered form it can be quite useful because it is more versatile. It can be turned into condensed milk or used double strength by halving the amount of water recommended on the packet. The liquid needed for reconstitution does not always have to be water. The pikelets recipe shows just how useful it is to have milk in a powdered form. For making curds (the most basic form of cheese) I have found the least sophisticated brands of powdered milk to be the most satisfactory. I suspect the up market brands contain 'something special' to prevent curdling. The consumer is not given much choice, just as it's hard to find a brand that does not contain the chemical for 'instant-mixing'.

# Galley-made Yoghurt

Yoghurt is a cultured dairy product adequately generated at home on board, in your own galley. I use a wide-necked, glass-lined thermos, bought on Nauru Island thirty years ago. Be wise enough to begin your homemade brewing with a good quality commercial yoghurt.

> **2 scant tablespoons mature yoghurt (from a previous batch or shop-bought)**
> **4 cups milk**

The temperature required for making yoghurt is 43°C. Preheat the thermos to roughly this temperature, remembering it is just above blood heat. Scald the milk and hold it at boiling point for five seconds to destroy unwanted bacteria. Allow the milk to cool down to roughly 43°C. Add the mature yoghurt to the scalded milk, close the thermos and brew for 6 to 8 hours. By suspending the thermos to counter the motion of the sea, you can avoid curds and whey separating as it brews.

# Curds

Curds, or cream cheese, are the simplest form of cheese-making. The skill of making curds is very useful in a galley where powdered milk is a staple, and refrigeration non-existent. Curds are formed by adding any sort of culinary acid — rennet (see below), vinegar, lemon or lime juice, citric acid or Epsom salts — to any strength of reconstituted powdered milk. (Buy only the cheapest brand of milk powder — upmarket brands may include an agent that prevents curdling.) Citric acid will give the curds a lemony flavour.

The curds can be used immediately for a dish such as sandesh, in cheesecakes and other sweet desserts, or they can be drained further for use as a savoury cottage cheese spread or dip.

**2 teaspoons vinegar (or other souring agent)**

**4 cups milk**

Take the milk to boiling point to sterilise it, holding it at boiling point for 3 seconds. Take it off the fire and let it cool to roughly blood heat, then stir in a little of your souring agent. Pause to see if curdling happens, and add a little more if needed. Different agents need different quantities.

Strain the curdled milk through a colander lined with a linen tea towel and reserve the liquid whey for scones, cakes or bread making.

# Rennet

Cheese is made by deliberately curdling milk and separating the solid curds from the liquid whey. The superior agent for achieving this curdling is rennet, obtained from the vell, or stomach, of calves; it makes a thick-textured curd. These days, rennet is easily obtained from supermarkets, where it is sold in white tablet form, sanitised, and far removed from its source. The disadvantage of rennet tablets for barefoot rovers is that they absorb moisture from the humidity of the climate and are soon rendered useless.

One substitute is the juice of the chardoon (*Scolymus cardunculus*) from the artichoke family, although these old-fashioned vegetables, no longer in vogue with commercial growers, are highly unlikely to be available to barefoot rovers unless they grow them themselves in their home gardens.

The lining of birds' giblets is another source of rennet. Unfortunately, giblets sold in supermarkets have already been emptied, and the lining containing the rennet has been separated and discarded. The giblets from my free ranging poultry in Broome measure three and a half inches across, and are heavily coated in rich, dark yellow fat. The coarse lining from such giblets (or from the giblets in guinea fowl, for instance) can be peeled away from the muscle, washed clear from its grain and other foodstuffs, then rubbed with cooking salt and allowed to dry.

When needed for cheese-making, take a dried piece and pour boiling water onto it, about half a cup of water onto one skin. Let it steep for 6 to 8 hours then use that water to prepare the milk for the cheese.

# Savoury Cottage Cheese

Curds can be compressed a little under a weight overnight. To compress the curds, leave them in the tea towel, standing in the colander; place a saucer on top (not resting on the colander) and on the saucer place a jam jar containing lead fishing sinkers.

> **curds**
>
> **caraway seed**
>
> **celery seed**
>
> **salt and pepper**
>
> **dry mustard powder (optional)**

These barefoot preservatives can be included in your cheese before the weight goes on top. This should keep for 48 hours.

# Pasta, pastry & dumplings

The simplest of equipment is all that's needed for top quality homemade pastry: a pudding basin and a knife. My cast-alloy Dutch oven, measuring 30 cm in diameter, sits atop a single metho stove, or pressure-kero burner, or in the coals of a shore fire, and faithfully turns out batch after batch of scones, bread, cakes, tarts, quiche, and pies.

Even with a Coolgardie Safe, or better still, a Barefoot Banana Safe (see page 249 for a blueprint), it is hardly possible to adhere to conventional advice to keep pastry ingredients cool, or let pastry rest. Instead, work quickly rather than too thoroughly; don't bother with a rolling pin, just coax the pastry into shape with your floury hands, pressing it out on the bench, or directly into the pie-plate.

Pastries and dumplings are meal-extenders. With good gravy made from good stock, and plenty of good suet pastry, I have received rapturous praise for feeding eight people on a total of 300g of meat in a beef stew.

# Gnocchi

Gnocchi is Italian for 'dumplings'. They often include potato, but don't have to. These gnocchi are so rich they make store-bought pasta pale into oblivion.

**1 cup butter**

**1 teaspoon salt**

**1 cup plain white flour**

**4 eggs**

**$^1/_2$ cup freshly grated parmesan cheese**

Bring the water, butter and salt to the boil. Take the saucepan off the heat and drop in all the flour, stirring until the paste comes away from the sides of the saucepan (like choux paste). Add the eggs, one at a time, blending it all into a rich, thick batter. Stir in the cheese. The gnocchi are then cooked in a large pot of swiftly boiling sea water. Flick snippets of batter deftly into the pot, using one teaspoon to cut off some batter and a second to scrape it into the boiling water. These gobbets of batter rise to the surface when cooked. Do them in batches rather than overcrowding the pot.

# Oatmeal Dumplings

$^1/_2$ cup plain flour

$^1/_4$ cup dripping

pinch of baking soda

$^1/_2$ cup rolled oats

1 onion finely chopped (about $^1/_2$ cup)

salt and pepper

Mix all the ingredients together, using a little milk to bind them into a paste. Quail-egg-sized pieces can then be dropped into a stew or soup to boil, or else one large dumpling can be cooked in a pudding cloth. For the latter, the cloth should be wetted and wrung out, then floured lightly before the paste is wrapped in it and tied securely with string. This parcel is then lowered into boiling salt water and kept boiling for 45 minutes, or 20 minutes under pressure in the pressure cooker.

# Polenta Dumplings

Polenta is coarse yellow cornmeal.

**1 cup flour**

**1 teaspoon salt**

**2 teaspoons baking powder**

**1 cup polenta**

**1 beaten egg**

**a little milk**

Mix the dry ingredients together, then add the beaten egg, using a knife to draw it together with enough milk to make dough. Using two teaspoons, cut out a teaspoonful and scrape it into boiling stock or soup. They rise to the surface when cooked and are ready to ladle into individual soup bowls.

# Semolina Pasta

**300 ml milk**

**1 tablespoon butter**

**a grating of nutmeg**

**salt and pepper**

**$^1/_2$ cup semolina**

**1 egg yolk**

Bring the milk to the boil with the butter, nutmeg, salt and pepper. Pour this into the top of the double boiler and, with water boiling hard in the bottom of the boiler, stir the semolina into the hot milk. Cover it and allow it to cook for about 15 minutes. Take it off the heat and add the egg yolk. Butter a large dish and spread the mixture into it. Leave it to cool enough to cut into forkable shapes and blend it into a bolognaise-style sauce.

Alternatively, cut it into biscuit-sized pieces, sprinkle with grated cheese and breadcrumbs, and bake lightly, to be served with fried fish.

# Short Pastry

Shortcrust pastry can be made with various flours and fats; only the proportions need to remain constant: you need twice as much flour as fat.

**200g plain flour**

**100g butter and/or lard**

**pinch of salt**

**2—3 tablespoons water**

**cream of tartar (or splash of lime juice or pinch of citric acid)**

Gather the ingredients into a paste that leaves the sides of the basin clean. Too much water will make pastry which is too wet. Discovering the correct amount of water is a matter of trial and error, since it depends on the particular water absorbency power of the flour.

A trace of acid such as cream of tartar increases the lightness of the dough.

# Suet Pastry

**1 cup fresh suet**

**2 cups of SR flour**

**¹/₂ teaspoon salt**

Grate the suet, add to it the SR flour and salt and use a knife to cut in enough water to make a paste which leaves the bowl clean. Don't knead it, just roll it out and get it into the oven fast before the baking powder in the flour dies. Suet pastry makes a hearty lid for any savoury pie; it also makes dumplings: quail-egg-sized pieces cooked for about 20 minutes at simmering point in the gravy of any stew.

Suet is the fat surrounding ox kidney. Less well known is flead, the fat surrounding the kidney of a pig, which makes exquisitely light pastry.
Flead comes from the slaughter in sheets of membrane & must be scraped off the membrane with a sharp knife. This is a tedious job but worth the effort.
Alternatively, you can boil up the flead & membrane in a large volume of water; the fat will separate & rise to the surface. What you can't do is use flead still in its membrane in your pastry, because flead membrane cooks into something strong enough to hoist the bosun's chair.

# Scone Lid

2 cups SR flour

1 tablespoon butter

$^1/_2$ teaspoon each of salt and pepper

$^1/_2$ cup water

No suet? No worries! Just draw together some scone dough out of flour, butter, salt and pepper, and enough water to form a soft dough. Coax it into the right shape to cover the surface of the stew and drop it onto the stew when the meat is nearly done. Continue cooking under the lid of the Dutch oven. Twenty minutes should see it ready.

It probably won't be neatly browned on top, but who cares? If you really want it to look brown, heating the lid of your Dutch oven super hot then plonking it on the stew would do the trick, but that's a lot of fuel just to have a prettily browned, conventional pie lid. On shore, hot coals piled onto the lid will brown the crust.

# Spud Pastry

1 cup cold mashed potato (or any mix of mashed potato, pumpkin,
  sweet potato, yam)

250g plain flour

120g fat (lard, beef dripping, or the fat from the gut of fish such as bluebone)

1 teaspoon salt

1 teaspoon baking powder

a little milk

Use the milk to draw all the ingredients together into a paste. Handle it lightly and use it to make 'sausage rolls' filled with any trimmings of cooked fish or veges or meat, or cheese and a little grated uncooked apple. Ten minutes in a hot oven should see them done.

# Vatruskat

Finnish-style vatruskat is very similar to spud pastry, but even simpler.

      **flour (e.g. barley flour)**

      **mashed potato**

      **cooked rice**

      **ghee**

      **black pepper**

Add enough flour to mashed potato to form dough. Roll out the dough into one sheet and cut it into 6–8 cm squares. These will be folded in half diagonally to enclose a filling in a triangular pastry.

Place some cooked rice, blended with a little ghee and black pepper, onto what will become the centre of each pasty. Fold the 'top half' over the filling and press the edges together. Bake in a hot Dutch oven or toast them on the girdle. Six minutes should see them done (the filling is already cooked).

# Condiments, sauces, dips & spreads

A cruising ship's galley is hardly the place for elaborate tableware and dinner services. Better to present food in a way that needs the least amount of fuss and equipment. Finger food, such as gobbets of cooked fish encased in spud pastry and vatruskat listed in the last chapter, or one-pot concoctions like Irish stew, make life easier.

Fish will frequently be on the galley menu, and the simplest and most nutritious way to cook it is to steam it. However, steamed fresh fish is often bland in flavour, so here too, sauces and condiments help offer variety. A condiment like dukkah finds its way onto cold fish, pickled eggs and even banana sandwiches.

# Dukkah

Dukkah is a Middle Eastern condiment, though it is far more than just a condiment. Served on bread that has been drizzled with olive oil it becomes a meal in itself. Dukkah is a very personal expression of the cook's delight in flavours. Secret combinations of seeds, nuts and spices are separately dry-roasted then pounded together to form a crushed mixture, but not a paste.

Traditionally, sesame seed forms the bulk of the mixture, and many recipes include dried mint and marjoram. My favourite blend mixes dried tart-flavoured rosella calyxes (*Hibiscus sabdariffa*) with celery seed, coriander seed, cumin, and the compulsory sesame seed and cashews.

The pestle and mortar gets lots of use making dukkah, and the resulting condiment may be as coarse or as fine as the cook feels inclined to prepare it. Off the cuff, a winning combination is the following:

> **250g sesame seed**
>
> **120g coriander seed**
>
> **120g cumin seed**
>
> **120g cashews**
>
> **1 dessertspoon celery seed**
>
> **1 dessertspoon dried rosellas**
>
> **salt and black pepper**

Dry-roast the sesame, coriander, cumin and cashews in separate batches. Why separate? Because they need different lengths of time to toast to the same crunchy brownness. Crush them and mix together with the remaining crushed ingredients.

# Sauces

Sauces are a boon for simplifying the preparation and presentation of food. A good sauce will draw together small and diverse bits and leftovers into one easily managed dish.

Fundamental white sauce is the classic example. This very basic sauce will happily take up any flavouring and bring together small tidbits and leftovers — cooked fish, grated cheese and cooked veges for instance.

Sauces are thickened by having flour cooked into them. The type of flour, and the proportion of flour to liquid, determines the thickness of the sauce. Cornflour, traditionally used in Asian recipes, contains twice as much starch as wheat flour, so the cook needs only half as much cornflour to thicken a sauce. See the discussion on the merits of cornflour and arrowroot on page 49.

Rule-of-thumb proportions for thickening with wheat flour (plain; white or wholemeal):

**1 tablespoon flour to 1 cup liquid = thin sauce**

**1$^1/_2$ tablespoons flour to 1 cup liquid = medium thick sauce**

**2 tablespoons flour to 1 cup liquid = thick sauce**

Begin by melting an amount of fat or oil equal to the amount of flour you intend to use; take it off the heat and stir in the flour to make a roux, then add the liquid. Keep stirring over the fire until all is blended, thickened and boiled.

Without butter or oil a sauce will still thicken, but it lacks the rich texture of creaminess in such classics as lobster mornay. In a recipe without butter or oil, such as for brandy sauce, the best choice of flour is cornflour.

# Classic White Sauce

Not surprisingly, white sauce is made with milk, however you may substitute fish-stock, the liquor inside oyster or pearlshell, water and a dash of wine, or vegetable stock — you don't have to waste anything edible! The genuine article also demands real butter, but ghee works as a substitute.

> 1½ tablespoons butter
>
> 1½ tablespoons plain white flour
>
> 1 cup hot milk
>
> ½ teaspoon salt

Using hot milk avoids lumps forming in the sauce, however, lumpy sauce is still edible!

Melt the butter gently in a saucepan. Take off the fire and add the flour, stirring it in to make a 'roux'. Blend in the hot milk, continue stirring and return to the fire. Stir carefully until it boils and thickens. Add salt and nutmeg and allow 2 minutes at close to boiling point for the flour to finish cooking.

# Barbecue Sauce

Mix together one tablespoon each of light molasses, prepared mustard and cider vinegar.

# Bread Sauce

Served especially with a whole fish that has been seasoned and wrapped in the bark of the cajebut paperbark tree (the bushie's culinary foil), and baked in a ground oven ashore.

     **1 onion, peeled and stuck with a few cloves (to make it easy to fish them out)**

     **1 blade of mace**

     **1 cup milk**

     **1 cup breadcrumbs, preferably white bread**

     **15g butter**

     **salt and pepper**

     **1 tablespoon cream or coconut cream**

Put the onion, cloves and mace into the milk and heat it in the double boiler. When the milk reaches the boil add the breadcrumbs, take the double boiler off the fire, and let the mixture steep for 20 minutes, kept very warm by the water in the bottom of the boiler. Remove the onion, cloves and mace; add the butter, salt and pepper and stir until the butter is melted and blended in. Make the sauce hot again and stir in the cream just before serving.

# Currant Sauce

30g currants

1 cup breadcrumbs

6 cloves

1 glass port wine

butter

From my great-great-grandmother Anne's recipe book, dated 1836, comes the Old Currant Sauce for Venison, wonderful with roo meat, camel meat or toothless old mutton as well.

*Boil an ounce of dried currants in half a pint (one cup) of water a few minutes; then add a small teacupful of breadcrumbs, six cloves, a glass of port wine, and a bit of butter. Stir it till the whole is smooth.*

This sauce, which is nearly a condiment, is equally good with hot or cold meat. The best bread to use is white bread or plain damper.

# Lemon Sauce

lemon

butter

Another of Anne's, dated 1836, a suitable accompaniment to fish that has been boiled in the pressure cooker.

*Cut thin slices of lemon into very small dice, and put them into melted butter; give it one boil, and pour it over boiled fowles.*

# Nam Coriander Chili Sauce

Sugar is the 'secret ingredient' of Vietnamese cooking.

2 cloves garlic

1 red chili

2 tablespoons sugar

$^1/_2$ cup chopped coriander leaves

flesh and juice of one lime

1 tablespoon Squid Brand fish sauce

With a pestle and mortar, pound the garlic and chili; add the sugar and coriander and continue beating to a smooth paste. Add the lime, pounding it all into a pulp with the fish sauce. Let it rest for a few minutes to develop the flavours, then use it as a dipping sauce with pieces of cooked seafood.

# Peanut Sauce

$1/4$ cup chopped onion

2 tablespoons peanut oil

$1/4$ teaspoon ground cardamom

$1/2$ cup smooth peanut butter

$1/4$ cup brown sugar

$1/4$ cup soy sauce

$1/4$ cup lemon juice

$1/4$ teaspoon tabasco (hot chili) sauce

Saute onion in peanut oil until transparent, stir in the cardamom and allow to cool. Blend peanut butter with remaining ingredients adding sugar first, and the sauteed onions last. Peanut sauce enriches plain steamed fish and rice.

# Brandy Sauce

To turn fruitcake into a lavish dessert.

3 rounded teaspoons cornflour

1 cup milk

30g sugar

brandy

Put the cornflour into a bowl. Measure out 1 cup of milk and use a little to blend the cornflour into a thin cream. Heat the remainder of the milk and dissolve the sugar in it. Pour the hot milk onto the cornflour mixture, stirring well, then return it all to the saucepan and stir it over the fire until it boils. Let it cool down a little before adding brandy in whatever proportion you fancy. If it's too hot the alcohol will evaporate.

## Dips & Spreads

# Anchoiade

If you happen to catch a glimpse of a red-hulled cat with the aerodynamics of a flying saucer as she whizzes past on the lightest of airs, likely as not she's the vessel *Songlines*, designed and built by Neville Lloyd and Caryl Plant. With her epoxied cedar-strip construction and wishbone rig, she is truly superb. Before *Songlines*, Neville and Caryl spent many years cruising aboard the Wharram cat *Jungai*.

Caryl traded some of my bread-sour for this recipe for anchoiade — delicious as a condiment or a sauce, it is traditionally spread onto thick slices of bread and toasted in a Dutch oven.

> **45g tin of anchovies, including the oil**
> **4 cloves garlic**
> **8 black olives**
> **1 small salad onion**
> **few drops red wine vinegar**
> **1 tablespoon chopped parsley**
> **1 ripe tomato (skinned)**

2 heaped teaspoons tomato puree

1 rounded teaspoon dried oregano

All you have to do is pound all the ingredients together into a paste.

# Barefoot Welsh Rarebit

Sauce or a spread, it's up to you.

30g butter

250g hard cheese, grated

1 teaspoon freshly made mustard

salt and pepper

2 or 3 tablespoons beer (or sima)

slices of toast or doorstops of bread

Start melting the butter and cheese in a heavy-based saucepan over a low heat. Add the mustard, salt and pepper, and finally the beer.

While it melts, prod it, poke it, chant spells and incantations over it *but don't stir it!* Serve it on toast as a spread.

# Hommous

**1 cup cooked chickpeas**

**1 cup sesame oil**

**$\frac{1}{2}$ teaspoon salt**

**$\frac{1}{2}$ cup raw sesame seed**

**1 dessertspoon tamarind juice (or fresh lemon or lime juice)**

Using a stone pestle and mortar, grind together the cooked chickpeas, sesame oil, salt and raw sesame seed. Add tamarind juice for a lemon flavour, or fresh lemon or lime juice.

# Taratoor (Tahini Spread)

**3 cloves fresh garlic**

**1 tablespoon tamarind juice (or fresh lemon juice)**

**$\frac{1}{2}$ cup sesame seeds**

**$\frac{1}{4}$ to $\frac{1}{2}$ cup olive oil**

**a little salt**

In a stone pestle and mortar pound the garlic with the tamarind juice. Crush and blend the sesame seed and olive oil (or use tahini) and mix this with the garlic. Transfer into a mixing bowl and, using a hand whisk, beat in enough cold water to make a mayonnaise texture. Add a sharpening of salt. This sauce is almost essential with falafel.

# Thirst quenchers

Drinks take on a new significance in the tropics. Dehydration is a real danger in an energetic outdoors lifestyle, in constantly high temperatures where even sunset does not significantly cool the air.

Drinks can quench your thirst and create a real perspiration (which provides refrigeration), or they can aggravate thirst. The hops in commercial beer, we are told, are essential for authentic flavour, but they contain a narcotic drug which serves to magnify my thirst. Carbonated drinks also aggravate my thirst. Hot tea (and also chili) promote a real perspiration, not just a sticky sweat. Perspiration allows the slightest movement of air to result in natural refrigeration. Blissful! Feel free to perspire liberally — it's the natural way to cool down in the tropics.

# Tea

My staunch favourite thirst quencher is tea. Tea is much more than just a drink — and it's much more than just a ritual.

One of my most deeply memorable cups of tea was brewed for me aboard the superbly elegant 47-foot Fyfe sloop *Carina*, originally *Awhanui IV*, launched in 1925. The first time I went aboard, Chris Blackwell and Polly Thompson had painstakingly restored the Fyfe, to the glorious enrichment of the internal timberwork, including a solid Blackwood cabin sole with an inlaid Huon pine grate, and an exquisite galley locker door whose leadlight glass pane bears an etching of the vessel herself.

The Fyfe was moored in Broken Bay in New South Wales and the still, icy cold of winter evening gloom was settling on the scene. Polly lit the antique Kopsen lamp in the galley and offered tea: Assam tea, black and strong, the flavour as unforgettable as the enfolding sanctuary of 'down below' aboard the Fyfe.

Years later, I myself was able to serve the same tea, in the same saloon, for the grandson of the builder of the Fyfe *Carina*, while listening to the family story of how the original owner, William Saxon, had taken delivery of the sloop just after being told he had a terminal illness, and not long to live. William Saxon was in command on her maiden voyage, taking the Fyfe from Sydney Harbour to Broken Bay. At the helm at night, mistakenly or deliberately, he gibed the yacht, stood up and was struck on the head by the massive boom. And thus he met his end.

For good quality tea you need good quality tea leaves and good quality water that is not laden with chlorine. The water must still be BOILING when it is poured onto the tea leaves.

Tea is not 'instant' — it is an infusion, and needs time for the infusion to unfold and release the best of its flavour. This is termed 'drawing' and takes four to five minutes. Once the tea has drawn, it must be poured off the tea leaves, or it will become 'over-drawn' and bitter in flavour.

Tea is not only refreshing: its high tannin content counterbalances the effects of fats in the diet such as suet, lard, butter, dripping and 'speck'. (Speck is a German speciality, a smoked bacon used in cooking to obtain smoke-flavoured lard.)

# Blaand

Blaand is an old-fashioned cold drink brewed from cottage cheese whey and probably made in every cottage household just a generation or two ago. It may be something of an acquired taste at first, but quickly becomes a compulsion, like sourdough bread, and is decidedly thirst-quenching.

Save the whey from cheese making and store it until fermentation begins. The length of time needed — 1 to 2 days — depends primarily on the temperature: the warmer the temperature, the faster it brews. Once sparkling, it is ready to drink and should be drunk within hours.

Beyond the sparkling stage it becomes flat and vinegary, but may be kept fermenting and sparkling by the regular addition of fresh whey. In fact, blaand works best when kept topped-up, like a sourdough culture, in what used to be termed a 'seasoned bottle'.

# Chili Cordial

Both tea and chili promote natural refrigeration by perspiration.

  **4 cups boiling water**

  **$^1/_2$ cup white sugar**

  **5 red chilies**

  **1 dessertspoon tamarind pulp**

  **$^1/_2$ teaspoon citric acid (or $^1/_4$ teaspoon cream of tartar and $^1/_4$ teaspoon tartaric acid)**

Pour the boiling water over the sugar, chilies, tamarind pulp and citric acid. Allow to steep until cool, then strain and bottle. Use with water or tonic water, or cold tea.

# Ginger Beer

Ginger beer is made from a ginger beer 'plant', which is a wild yeast growing in a solution of water, sugar and ginger. The wild yeast can originate from fruit such as mulberries, or the skin of dates or raisins. Muscatels seem to be the only raisins not coated in oil by manufacturers wanting to prevent the bloom of yeast forming. The easiest kind of ginger to use is the dried and powdered form.

  **To start the plant you need:**

  **6 raisins with a visible bloom of yeast, seen as a light powder on the surface**

  **a generous half cup of fresh lemon or lime juice**

  **1 teaspoon mashed lemon or lime flesh**

  **2 teaspoons powdered ginger**

**4 teaspoons white sugar**

**2 cups cold water**

Mix these ingredients together in a glass jar of three-cup capacity with a screw top. Lightly
the jar to exclude other unwanted yeasts and leave it in a warm place to begin fermenting
warmer the weather the faster it will get going. After three days or so, bubbles should in
fermentation. Feed the plant daily with 2 teaspoons of ginger and 4 teaspoons of sugar. /
week, streams of bubbles should be visible rising from the bottom, indicating a strong p

**To make the beer:**

**4 cups boiling water**

**4 cups white sugar**

**2 cups fresh lemon or lime juice**

**7 litres cold water**

**the liquid from the ginger beer plant jar**

Boil 4 cups of water and add the sugar, stirring until it dissolves. Take off the fir
lemon or lime juice. In a bucket large enough to hold all the ingredients, mix tog
water and the syrup of sugar water and juice. Add the liquid from the plant, stra
muslin cloth. Save the strained culture for the next plant. Bottle the beer in ster
leaving plenty of headroom. It will be ready to drink in two weeks.

The culture from the strained plant can be divided in half, mixed with 2 cu
and grown as two separate plants, fed as before with sugar and ginger daily.

# Kambotscha

Also known as the 'Tea Beast', kambotscha is a yeast bacteria mix (*Acetobacter aceti*, ssp. *xylinum*) that creates excellent cold drinks from waste tea and is wonderful thirst quencher for adults and children alike. The drink is 'sub-acid' and is credited with great folk-medicine potency as it eliminates toxins through the digestive process, reputedly beating the tropical aggressor tinea when consumed twice a day in 100-ml doses!

Bill Mollison's *Permaculture Book of Ferment and Human Nutrition*, which will doubtless find its way into every barefoot library, describes the Beast and how to use it, though there is no recipe for the culture itself: you have to acquire a piece of the 'tough, membranous, fibrous mat' yourself somehow.

Put some of the culture in a large wide-mouthed preserving jar and fill up with tea, adding 100g of sugar per litre of liquid when cool. In the tropics this culture brews fast. Depending on just how acidic you like it, it may be ready after five days; leave it longer if you wish. If left for four weeks or so, a strong vinegar is produced which is a good substitute for cider vinegar in pickles, salad dressings and soused fish.

The culture will grow to fit the diameter of the container, and floats above the tea in time. separates in sheets and is split up every 3—4 weeks to start the process again with fresh jars. inger or other spices could be added on bottling when the matured solution is drained off the bbery culture mat. Ideally kambotscha should be stored under refrigeration, but sterilising it by ding it at boiling point for 5 seconds will greatly increase its shelf-life without refrigeration.

# Lassi

Lassi is simply lashings of galley-made yoghurt stirred into cold water, in whatever proportions suit the drinker or the cook. It can be sharpened with a dash of cider vinegar and salt, or sweetened with sugar or honey.

# Lime Cordial

Homemade lime cordial comes a close second to tea in the refreshment stakes and is dream-easy to make and store. Simple, homemade fruit juice is turned into cordial concentrate by boiling with sugar and water and citric acid (or tartaric or salicylic acid). Citric acid has the best flavour.

> **4 cups fresh limejuice**
>
> **2 kg white sugar**
>
> **30g citric acid**
>
> **4 cups water**
>
> **1 tablespoon crushed coriander seed**

Boil all the ingredients together briskly for 10 minutes, then seal in sterilised bottles. This quantity fills four empty 700 ml gin bottles. It's a tough life when the cook must empty the gin bottles to have them ready for the cordial!

Serve diluted with water, cold tea or tonic water, or use it neat to dress up fruit salad or stewed fruit.

Other fresh fruit juices make equally good cordial, for example orange (and cloves), passionfruit (boil up the skins as well, then strain it), and grapefruit (with mace). Just keep the proportions the same.

# Pirr

Pirr is a traditional Scottish drink that provides instant energy to a flagging watch. Note that the oatmeal is very fine, like attar flour: it is not rolled oats.

**2 tablespoons oatmeal**

**1 teaspoon sugar**

**$1/4$ teaspoon cream of tartar**

**milk to blend**

**1 cup boiling water**

Mix the oatmeal, sugar and cream of tartar in a jug and add just enough cold milk to blend into a smooth paste. Pour in the boiling water, stirring quickly. Drink hot or cold.

# Sima

Sima is a Finnish ale brewed in the bottle. Clean 1 litre or 1.25 litre plastic cool-drink bottles with plastic screw-top lids are suitable. You can get new lids from a home-brew supplier or re-use the original lid after soaking in hot water.

**5 litres water**

**2 lemons**

**250g white sugar**

**250g brown sugar**

**200 ml honey**

**1 tablespoon bread-sour or 1 sachet (8g) freeze-dried yeast**

**raisins**

Pare off the lemon peel and put it in a large saucepan — preferably of stainless steel. Separate the pith from the flesh; discard the pith (yeth!) and chop the flesh. Add the flesh and juice to the peel; add also the sugars and honey. Boil the water and pour it over the contents of the saucepan. Let it dissolve the sugars and cool to blood heat. Now add the sour or yeast, and let it brew overnight. Drop one or two raisins into each empty bottle. Fill the bottles with beer, but leave plenty of headroom. Cap and seal. Traditionally, the brew is ready when the raisins have risen to the surface, after about two days.

# Splice the Mainbrace: alcoholic drinks

In days past, when ships sailed round Cape Horn on voyages lasting years, 'splice the mainbrace' was the term used for repairing the most essential component of the standing-rigging of the vessel. Everyone's life depended on the success of this job, and so the most able and most courageous seaman was picked for the task. To increase his enthusiasm he was awarded an extra tot of rum.

Somehow, without trivialising the reverence due to such heroic endeavours, today's meaning of the term has become an excuse for indulging in alcohol. Since it is quite scandalously uncivilised to indulge in alcohol earlier than 1800 hrs, what a comfort it is to study enough navigation to understand that, at any given time, it must be 1800 hrs somewhere on the globe, so all one really needs to do is navigate successfully to the drinks locker.

# Athol Brose

A Scottish tradition dating from 1475.

**1 cup prepared oatmeal (not rolled oats)**

**4 dessertspoons honey (heather or Tasmanian leatherwood, or, Kimberley**

**'blackberry honey' from a native fig tree)**

**whisky to make 1 litre**

To prepare the oatmeal, put it into a bowl and mix with cold water to the consistency of a thick paste. Let it steep for about 30 minutes, then pass it through a colander lined with cheesecloth, wringing it out to extract all the cream and leave the oatmeal as dry as possible. Set aside the meal and use the cream to blend with the honey. Traditionally, this must be stirred with a pure silver spoon, then stored in a quart bottle, adding whisky to fill the bottle. Shake it carefully before serving as a liqueur with coffee. A tropical touch is to serve it blended half and half with coconut cream.

# Barefoot Beer

The main utensil used for this brew on *Banana Mousskourri* is an old aluminium bucket originally designed for heating milk to make clotted cream and pouring it safely. It has one handle like a bucket handle, and another, made of bakelite, opposite a spout on the rim.

A batch of this brew is ready to drink after just a couple of days.

**1 ½ cups sugar**

**half litre malt**

1 tablespoon dried hops (optional)

5 litres boiling water

1 dessertspoon active bread-sour or 1 sachet (8g) freeze-dried yeast

Put the sugar, malt and hops into the bucket. Bring the water to the boil and pour it into the bucket. Stir it up well. Let it cool to blood heat, then add the yeast (remembering that the yeast will die if the temperature is too high). Let this stand and ferment for one day, loosely covered with a towel. Strain it into clean plastic soft-drink bottles, with new sealable lids. Stand it somewhere relatively cool, such as in the bilge. It is ready to drink on the following day. Yes, it's mildly alcoholic.

# Koumiss

Koumiss is essentially an alcoholic lassi. It is best served in tall glasses filled with ice. Like lassi it can be sweetened with honey or sharpened with salt. Make a double batch because you will probably want to trade some of it for some ice from your neighbouring cruising boat!

1 dessertspoon bread-sour (or 8g sachet freeze-dried yeast)

2 tablespoons sugar

4 cups warm milk

Blend all the ingredients together in a clean plastic 1.25 litre screw-top soft-drink bottle and close the lid tightly.

North of 18°S this brews fast on the bench. After 6 to 8 hours all is transformed into a frothy, fizzy drink with an alcoholic content similar to beer.

# Lamb's Wool

Drink this hot or cold.

> 1 cooking apple
>
> 1 cup milk
>
> sugar
>
> beer or sweet white wine
>
> nutmeg

Roast a cooking apple and whip the pulp in a glass of milk until it is frothy. Next, a shandy is made by adding sugar and beer or sweet white wine. A grating of nutmeg will not only improve the flavour, it actually increases the effect of the alcohol.

# Rum Sillabub

In port, or having just left a port somewhere, fresh stores will probably include fresh cream. Cream tastes extra good when you haven't had any for a while. This recipe for six people is conventionally a dessert and includes a hefty dollop of fresh cream. It's listed here because of its wickedly high proportion of rum, preferably Bundy. Australian children, from one end of the nation to the other, have delighted in chorusing the lusty refrain: 'Bundaberg Rum is a very fine rum; Bundaberg Rum will grow hairs on your BUM!'

150 ml rum

juice and grated rind of 4 fresh limes (say ½ cup)

100g pure icing sugar

1 cup whipping cream

Mix together the rum, limejuice, rind-zest and sugar. Start to whip the cream, and add the rum mixture a little at a time, beating each addition in thoroughly. When it's all whipped up, simply dollop it into individual servings and enjoy it with sweet wafer biscuits.

# Van Der Hum

This liqueur is traditionally made in Madagascar with naartjies, a fruit similar to tangerines. A suitable substitute is cumquats or mandarins. This recipe was written out for me by my Broome friend and Tai Chi instructor Angela Bakker. At one stage at home aboard the 32-foot steel sloop *Micropus*, Angela now makes her art and pottery and home in Broome, where she not only fires her own pots, but first collects and prepares the clay from local Kimberley deposits.

6 cloves

half a nutmeg, grated

1 stick cinnamon

750 ml brandy

25 ml citrus fruit (naartjies are best), sliced finely

60 ml rum

Lightly bruise the spices and tie them in a bag to make it easy to fish them out later. Place all the ingredients in a large bottling jar (at least 1 litre capacity) and leave for a month, stored out of direct sunlight. Turn the bottle from time to time to blend it well.

After a month, or longer if convenient, strain the contents through muslin. Discard the bag of spices and add a syrup made by boiling together 125 ml of water and 125g sugar until thick.

Re-bottle and cork. Make sure the syrup is cool before adding it, or the alcohol will be destroyed.

# Food Safety in the Tropics

Without getting embroiled in arguments about contamination such as mercury in fish, DDT and radioactive strontium residues, and unsuitable food-packaging, a few observations can be made about avoiding food poisoning in the ship's galley.

World-wide, food poisoning commonly results from contamination by certain bacteria, especially staphylococci and salmonella.

Different lifestyles associated with different cultures result in different tolerance levels of these common bacteria. For example, the local people of Bali thrive on their island with their own local water supply and cuisine, yet the same water and food often produces a dose of 'Bali Belly' (gastroenteritis) in tourists from other countries.

The degree of poisoning depends on the tolerance level of the eater and on the length of time the bacteria have had to multiply in the contaminated food.

Bacteria thrive in warm temperatures (15° to 60°C) and can replicate themselves every twenty minutes. At temperatures as low as a domestic refrigerator (below 4°C) bacteria become dormant, but remain alive. Heated to temperatures above 65°C they are destroyed, but the toxins produced by staphylococci are not destroyed and remain toxic.

Bacteria also thrive in moisture, or liquid, such as meat-juice, milk or water. A moisture content of below 35 per cent directly inhibits their growth. Thus dry food such as dried apricots and dates, uncooked rice or navy beans, are poor hosts for such bacteria, as are foods preserved in salt, sugar or vinegar. Protein foods like raw meat, raw fish, milk and moist cooked foods, left standing too long, are perfect hosts.

How, then, can these unwanted bacteria be kept under control and at tolerable levels on board a refrigeration-free sailing boat cruising in areas where the average temperature, night and day, falls well within the range of 15°C-40°C?

In a word, the answer is hygiene. With the aid of sterilising powder (available from home-brew suppliers), commonsense galley practice in food hygiene includes scrupulously clean hands and utensils, careful menu planning, and the systematic avoidance of cross-contamination through carelessness.

Don't even think of bringing more raw meat into the galley than can be safely handled, prepared, bottled under pressure, or consumed in one meal. Don't mix up more powdered milk than can be used immediately. Plan to prepare too little food for a meal rather than too much. Try not to have any leftovers to worry about, and most certainly don't leave leftovers lying around for any length of time.

There is also a folk-theory which is worth mentioning here: it tells us that if a kitchen environment is a good, busy host to beneficial bacteria, such as those cultured in bread-sour and yoghurt, then these 'goodies' tend to elbow-out the nasty unwanted strains. Let's hope so!

Except for botulism, the following are usually mild forms of food poisoning and the suggested remedy is to fast for 12 hours, drinking only boiled water or tea. Prevention is much better than cure.

## Staphylococcus aureus

*Staphylococcus aureus* — or golden staph — poisoning is caused by a toxin produced by the bacteria. These bacteria exist on human skin and are most commonly spread to food by sneezing or coughing, and through direct handling of foods with dirty hands. A distinction of this bacterium is that it can tolerate higher levels of salt than other bacteria, and multiplies in commercial ham and small goods, as well as other protein foods like custards and cream.

The toxins it produces are heat-resistant and freeze-resistant and very hard to destroy. It is ingestion of the toxins, not the live bacteria, which causes poisoning. Symptoms of golden staph poisoning — diarrhoea, vomiting and stomach cramps — arise a couple of hours after eating contaminated food.

As with all bacteria, avoid cross-contamination: wash the knife you used to cut the ham before dipping it into the ghee.

## Salmonella

Salmonella poisoning is more common than staphylococcus, and is caused by ingesting the live bacteria, commonly found in raw meat, commercial poultry meat, and commercial sausages. Typically, poisoning occurs when protein foods have been contaminated by unwashed hands, by insect or rodent excreta, or by flies. Seafood from polluted waters is also a well-known source of salmonella poisoning, as is the gut of domestic chickens raised in intensive-farming systems.

Symptoms of salmonella poisoning are similar to *Staphylococcus aureus*, but the incubation period — the length of time before symptoms show up — is around 24 hours.

The bacteria are easily destroyed by heat. If you think the meat or fish is not fresh enough, cook it long and hard to destroy the bacteria.

# Clostridium perfingens

*Clostridium perfingens* causes less severe poisoning symptoms, commonly nausea and stomach upset showing up after about 12 hours. This is a common result of commercial takeaway food left warming too long and restaurants where stews and roasts are cooked one day and warmed up on following days.

The bacteria are found in the intestinal tract of humans and animals and spores can withstand boiling, steaming, stewing, or braising for up to 5 hours.

Adequate personal hygiene, and the ruthless elimination of insects and rodents from food storage areas, are essential to conquer this health threat. Also, extreme care is needed when drawing a carcass, to avoid puncturing the gut and contaminating the flesh.

# Bacillus cereus

*Bacillus cereus* needs a special mention because rice is such a common staple aboard cruising boats. This bacterium originates in the soil, but can be found in cereals, especially rice where it is protected by the presence of starch. Its spores can withstand near-boiling temperatures. Cooked moist rice left standing too long is a perfect host in tropical weather.

# Botulism

Botulism is the most serious form of food poisoning and was the 'big bad bogey-man' of home-preserved food until certain facts were identified. Most cases of botulism food poisoning are identified because they have been fatal! Don't be too alarmed though: very few cases have been recorded in Australia.

Symptoms are blurred vision, slurred speech, inability to hold up the head, and eventual respiratory arrest unless the victim is given help to breathe until medication can reverse the progress of the poisoning.

Botulism is present in soil, and may even be present in produce grown hydroponically. This means that when anyone grows or buys carrots, for example, it is possible (if only remotely) that the carrots contain the bacteria. If the carrots are cooked at a brisk boil for 15 minutes the bacteria are destroyed and the carrots are safe to eat. Similarly, if the carrots are preserved by the pressure cooker method using the correct equipment, pressure, temperature and length of time (see below), bacteria will be destroyed and the produce remain contamination-free for many months. But if procedures are not followed exactly, the bacteria may continue to multiply inside the sealed bottle, and a long storage time may allow a lethal concentration to emerge. Once again: prevention is better than cure.

The botulism bacterium thrives best in the middle range of temperatures (15° to 60°C), in the **absence of air** and in a very **moist** environment, most commonly in a tin of processed food. The spores produce a very powerful toxin and are extremely durable at high temperatures.

Spores are **destroyed** by **pressure cooker home-bottling** methods using at least 10 lbs pressure. The toxin is destroyed by brisk boiling and 116°C temperature for 15 minutes.

Don't sample suspect food until it has been boiled. If, during boiling, it froths and foams and smells foul, destroy it immediately; don't even feed it to the hermit crabs.

With sophisticated navigation equipment now commonplace on even the most modest of vessels, small boats and ordinary people are able to navigate further and further away from community back-up, necessitating a greater need for self-reliance in the realm of nutrition and health. Accidents can happen anywhere, and what would we do without the Royal Flying Doctor Service? But an understanding of basic food safety and the importance of freshness in food will avoid the woes of food poisoning or the need to radio for a medivac on that score. Even the spartan standards aboard the trusty old Wharram *Juringa* — which has no autohelm, generator, engine or outboard, and no access to the www or to weatherfax — allow for a modest Global Positioning System, used to confirm dead reckoning.

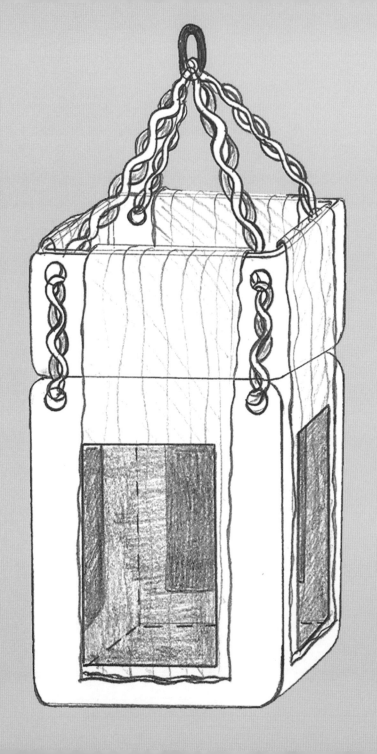

# Barefoot Banana Safe

In the goldfields of Western Australia, our pioneering forebears ingeniously devised the Coolgardie Safe, a metal wire-screened box which served as a fridge by means of water siphoning down onto wet canvas draped over the sides. When a breeze blew onto it the temperature inside the box was significantly lowered.

The same principle is used to make a Barefoot Banana Safe, with two 25-litre plastic square drums lashed one on top of the other. Telstra uses such drums to replenish the battery-water supply in solar-powered energy sites throughout the Kimberley, and discards them once the water has been used.

Cut the top half off the top drum so that the remaining bottom half serves as the reservoir of water. Water will siphon down over the sides of the bottom drum, in which food is stored.

Prepare the bottom drum by cutting out a panel on each of its four sides. Replace the panels on three of the sides by lacing pieces of hessian, cut on the cross, over the panel openings. On the fourth side make an access door using hessian hinged along the top with lacing, loose on the sides, and weighted with lead split shot along the bottom to stay 'shut'. Split shot is available from fishing tackle suppliers.

To lash the drums together, holes need to be drilled in both. In the bottom drum, on the side with the door, drill a hole above the top left-hand corner of the door and another above the top right-hand corner. Next, drill two holes in the corresponding positions on the side opposite the door. In the reservoir drum, drill four holes in corresponding positions near the top rim. The closer the holes are to the rim, the more water it will be possible to hold in the reservoir.

Lash the bottom to the top in two 'handles'. Begin with a figure-eight knot inside the bottom drum, lead the lashing outside and up to the top drum, inside and across for the first handle, then out, down, and in to the bottom drum, ending with another figure-eight knot. Make a second handle parallel to the first. You may decide to make both handles out of one length of line. Make the loops of the handles long enough to join in a shackle so the safe can be hung in the shade. The loops must be the same length to keep the unit level.

Cut two long lengths of hessian (or cotton towelling or canvas — basically any fabric that will absorb water) the same width as the base of the reservoir. Place one length of fabric across the other, at right angles, to form a cross. Place the overlapping parts of the cross in the bottom of the reservoir and drape the fabric up over the rim of the reservoir and down over the four sides of the safe below, where it can be tied together with a small length of line. A dive-weight holds the fabric under the water in the reservoir.

Fill the reservoir with sea water and it will soon begin to siphon down the fabric.

At anchor, the Barefoot Banana Safe is hung in the silence of the shade beneath the slatted decking built between the two hulls of the cat. No 12V or 240V fridge problems, no refrigeration mechanic to pay, no need for a generator and its inevitable noise, no fuel costs, no pollution, no stress and no breakdowns! Just peace and quiet to enjoy.

# Conversion Tables

Most of the recipes offered in *Barefoot Roving* are old, and came to me in imperial measure. These have all been converted into approximate metric measures, where:

1 gill = half a cup

1 pint = just under 500 ml or half a litre = 2 cups

2 pints = 1 quart = just under 1 litre = 4 cups

16 ounces (oz) = 1 pound (lb) = roughly 500g (half a kilo)

8 oz = approximately 250g

4 oz = approximately 120g

1 oz = approximately 30g

1 cup = 250 ml

Unless specified otherwise, teaspoon and tablespoon measures are level.

Most galley ovens don't have a thermostat, so temperatures are given in descriptive terms. Here are the equivalents in °C and °F:

|          | °C  | °F  |
|----------|-----|-----|
| cool     | 120 | 250 |
| slow     | 135 | 275 |
| warm     | 165 | 325 |
| moderate | 175 | 350 |
| hot      | 220 | 425 |
| very hot | 230 | 450 |

# Bibliography

Burbury, Mary 1833, Letter printed in the *Coventry Herald*, copy held by the British Museum Newspaper Library, Colindale, UK.

Colwell, Max 1995, *Whaling around Australia*. Seal Books Lansdowne.

Downes, John 1983, *The Natural Tucker Bread Book*. Hyland House.

Ewald, Ellen Buchman 1973, *Recipes for a Small Planet*. Ballantine Books.

Hepworth, A. (nd), *Liklik Buk*. Lae Information Centre, PO Box 793, Lae, PNG.

Hordern, Marsden 1997, *King of the Australian coast*. Melbourne University Press.

Mollison, Bill 1993, *The Permaculture Book of Ferment and Human Nutrition*. Tagari Publications.

Royal Flying Doctor Service 1973, *Mantle of Safety Cookbook 2*. Australia: Hyde Park Press.

Robertson, Dougal 1973, *Survive the Savage Sea*. Great Britain: Elek Books.

Robertson, Laurel, Carol Flinders & Bronwen Godfrey 1978, *Laurel's Kitchen*. Nilgiri Press.

Wightman, Glenn & Andrews, Milton 1991, *Bush Tucker Identikit*. Conservation Commission of the Northern Territory.

# Biographical Note

Sylvia Lerch is a passionate barefoot rover from way back, and boats keep bobbing up in her 'roving profile'. She has been an oyster farmer, a restaurateur, teacher, food hygiene instructor, taxidermist and free-range egg producer. Some of her recipes go as far back as her great-great-grandmother Anne, newly arrived in Van Dieman's Land in the early 1800s.

# Index

First published 2005 by
FREMANTLE ARTS CENTRE PRESS
25 Quarry Street, Fremantle
(PO Box 158, North Fremantle 6159)
Western Australia.
www.facp.iinet.net.au

Consultant Editor Janet Blagg
Designer Adrienne Zuvela
Back cover image Frances Andrijich
Production Vanessa Bradley
Typeset by Fremantle Arts Centre Press
Printed by Craft Print International


National Library of Australia
Cataloguing-in-publication data

Lerch, Sylvia.
Barefoot roving: the travelling kitchen.

ISBN 1 920731 98 9.

1. Outdoor cookery.  I. Fremantle Arts Centre Press.
II. Title.

641.578